YOSEMITE CLIMBS

BIG WALLS

YOSEMITE CLIMBS

BIG WALLS

Don Reid

Chockstone Press
Evergreen, Colorado

YOSEMITE CLIMBS: BIG WALLS

ISBN 0-934641-54-4

Published and distributed by
Chockstone Press, Inc.
Post Office Box 3505
Evergreen, Colorado 80437-3505

Front cover: Peter Takeda, Pitch 14 on *Sunkist*, El Capitan. Photo by Greg Epperson.

Back cover: Royal Robbins lounges on El Cap Spire. Photo by Tom Frost.

All uncredited photos by George Meyers.

Table of Contents

WARNING: CLIMBING IS A SPORT WHERE YOU MAY BE SERIOUSLY INJURED OR DIE.
READ THIS BEFORE YOU USE THIS BOOK.

This guidebook is a compilation of unverified information gathered from many different climbers. The author cannot assure the accuracy of any of the information in this book, including the topos and route descriptions, the difficulty ratings, and the protection ratings. These may be incorrect or misleading and it is impossible for any one author to climb all the routes to confirm the information about each route. Also, ratings of climbing difficulty and danger are always subjective and depend on the physical characteristics (for example, height), experience, technical ability, confidence and physical fitness of the climber who supplied the rating. Additionally, climbers who achieve first ascents sometimes underrate the difficulty or danger of the climbing route out of fear of being ridiculed if a climb is later down-rated by subsequent ascents. Therefore, be warned that you must exercise your own judgment on where a climbing route goes, its difficulty and your ability to safely protect yourself from the risks of rock climbing. Examples of some of these risks are: falling due to technical difficulty or due to natural hazards such as holds breaking, falling rock, climbing equipment dropped by other climbers, hazards of weather and lightning, your own equipment failure, and failure of fixed protection.

You should not depend on any information gleaned from this book for your personal safety; your safety depends on your own good judgment, based on experience and a realistic assessment of your climbing ability. If you have any doubt as to your ability to safely climb a route described in this book, do not attempt it.

The following are some ways to make your use of this book safer:

1. **CONSULTATION:** You should consult with other climbers about the difficulty and danger of a particular climb prior to attempting it. Most local climbers are glad to give advice on routes in their area and we suggest that you contact locals to confirm ratings and safety of particular routes and to obtain first-hand information about a route chosen from this book.

2. **INSTRUCTION:** Most climbing areas have local climbing instructors and guides available. We recommend that you engage an instructor or guide to learn safety techniques and to become familiar with the routes and hazards of the areas described in this book. Even after you are proficient in climbing safely, occasional use of a guide is a safe way to raise your climbing standard and learn advanced techniques.

3. **FIXED PROTECTION:** Many of the routes in this book use bolts and pitons which are permanently placed in the rock. Because of variances in the manner of placement, weathering, metal fatigue, the quality of the metal used, and many other factors, these fixed protection pieces should always be considered suspect and should always be backed up by equipment that you place yourself. Never depend for your safety on a single piece of fixed protection because you never can tell whether it will hold weight.

Be aware of the following specific potential hazards which could arise in using this book:

1. **MISDESCRIPTIONS OF ROUTES:** If you climb a route and you have a doubt as to where the route may go, you should not go on unless you are sure that you can go that way safely. Route descriptions and topos in this book may be inaccurate or misleading.

2. **INCORRECT DIFFICULTY RATING:** A route may, in fact be more difficult than the rating indicates. Do not be lulled into a false sense of security by the difficulty rating.

3. **INCORRECT PROTECTION RATING:** If you climb a route and you are unable to arrange adequate protection from the risk of falling through the use of fixed pitons or bolts and by placing your own protection devices, do not assume that there is adequate protection available higher just because the route protection rating indicates the route is not an "X" or an "R" rating. Every route is potentially an "X" (a fall may be deadly), due to the inherent hazards of climbing, including, for example, failure of fixed protection, your own equipment's failure, or improper use of climbing equipment.

THERE ARE NO WARRANTIES, WHETHER EXPRESS OR IMPLIED, THAT THIS GUIDEBOOK IS ACCURATE OR THAT THE INFORMATION CONTAINED IN IT IS RELIABLE. THERE ARE NO WARRANTIES OF FITNESS FOR A PARTICULAR PURPOSE OR THAT THIS GUIDE IS MERCHANTABLE. YOUR USE OF THIS BOOK INDICATES YOUR ASSUMPTION OF THE RISK THAT IT MAY CONTAIN ERRORS AND IS AN ACKNOWLEDGEMENT OF YOUR OWN SOLE RESPONSIBILITY FOR YOUR CLIMBING SAFETY.

PREFACE

The discovery of Yosemite Valley continues. Experiencing the natural beauty of this valley is timeless and has inspired generations. Each generation has found new facets of exploration within this incomparable valley.

The number of climbing routes has once again expanded significantly since the last edition of Yosemite Climbs. In an effort to maintain a guidebook of practical size for both the user and publisher, the information is now being presented in two volumes: a Big Wall guide and a Free Climbing guide. Although each book will be more focused and manageable, categorizing climbing routes in this manner has some shortcomings. For example on the west face of El Capitan or the Chouinard-Herbert or Sentinel Rock where once big wall technique was the norm, contemporary mainstream climbers are more often dealing with a chalk bag rather than a haul bag. Although other big routes such as **Lurking Fear**, **The Nose**, and **Zodiac** on El Capitan; the **South Face Route** and **The Prow** of Washington Column; the **Regular Northwest Face** route on Half Dome, etc. are now climbed in a day with increasing regularity, most parties still pursue a multi-day, haul and jümar, traditional big wall game plan. Conversely, free or mostly free routes that are particularly long, involved, and difficult such as **Escape from Freedom** on Mt. Watkins and **Southern Belle** and **Karma** on Half Dome may require days. On these routes, bivys, haulbags and an atmosphere or big wall logistics interceeds. In the end, the individual climber, and not a big wall or free climbing guidebook, will determine the most realistic format of ascent.

As in the previous books, a number of Yosemite's climbs have been excluded, mostly pre-1970 in origin and of dubious interest to contemporary climbers. The *1971 Climber's Guide to Yosemite Valley*, written by Steve Roper and published by the Sierra Club, is a valuable archive of information for these routes.

The introduction material has been greatly expanded in this edition. John Dill provided a valuable and illuminating analysis of the serious climbing accidents that have occurred in the park since 1970.

The topos are the result of compiling route information from many sources. Those climbers who provided information for previous editions of this guide are to be thanked again; they helped build the framework for this book. Once again, many people were generous with their time by providing detailed lists of corrections to the previous work, and many others unselfishly shared with the authors information about their new routes. This guide is clearly the result of a group effort. Of particular note are the following people who devoted an extraordinary amount of time and effort to ensure that this guide is as accurate as possible: Dave Bengston, Steve Bosque, Eric Brand, Walter Flint, Kevin Fosburg, Tucker Tech, Russ Walling and Brad Young. Special thanks to Eric Kohl and Walt Shipley.

The authors wish to acknowledge and thank the United States Geological Survey for the map of Yosemite Valley (1:24,000 scale) that has been reproduced at the back of this book.

While all uncredited photos were taken by George Meyers, the authors wish to thank the National Park Service, and particularly John Dill, for the use of their photos, some taken from perspectives impossible to duplicate without a helicopter.

There will be errors in this book. It is requested that corrections, as well as new route information, be sent to the author care of Chockstone Press, PO Box 3505, Evergreen, Colorado 80439.

Sixth pitch of **Son of Heart** (aka **Heart Woute**), El Capitan. Photo: Dave Schultz, Walter J. Flint Collection.

INTRODUCTION

Yosemite Valley continues to reveal itself as an incomparably beautiful and vast rock-sculptured wonder. Decade after decade, it has been an inspiring dream for climbers, and has also provided the fulfilling reality of a supreme granite-climbing experience. The number of climbers attracted to Yosemite, and the level of drama played out in this arena, is testimony to Yosemite's allure, as is the sheer number of routes established by these climbers.

Hundreds of rock climbing areas have been developed around the world in the last 100 years, yet none have so fired the imagination of climbers, or meant so much to the high standards of contemporary mountaineering, as Yosemite Valley. As a result, the Valley has taken on an increasingly international flavor as thousands of climbers from around the world have traveled here to climb. Fun-in-the-sun rock climbing is what Yosemite is all about, but it is more than just a crag area: it is a complicated valley, with the many cliff formations placed in such a way as to require of the climber some greater mountaineering skills.

Located 150 miles east of San Francisco, Yosemite Valley is the dramatic centerpoint of Yosemite National Park,. Although only seven square miles in size, it contains some of North America's most exquisite scenery and is popular with tourists: millions of people visit the park each year, though primarily in summer. While the Valley remains the traffic center for this 1,200-square mile park for both tourist and climber alike, the intricate terrain provides adequate cover for the rock climber wishing to lose sight of the tourists and gain some sense of a wilderness experience. Not all climbers adopt this option, of course, and in full season roadside crags are often crowded.

Direct flights can be taken to Los Angeles or San Francisco from most major cities of the world. Buses travel regularly to the nearby cities of Fresno and Merced, and on to Yosemite, albeit somewhat inconveniently. Hitchhiking is commonly successful in California, especially for those prepared with destination signs and interesting-looking climbing paraphernalia.

When to Come

The best time to climb in Yosemite is during the months of April and May, September and October. Pleasant temperatures, lack of summertime tourist crowds, and the fact that the waterfalls are in their full glory make the spring the most popular time for climbers. April can be pretty rainy, however. Autumn is usually quieter and normally has great climbing weather, but the days are short and it can storm just about anytime. Summer sees most of the local climbers heading to Yosemite's high country domes at Tuolumne Meadows to escape the heat. In spite of occasional 100°F temperatures in summer, climbing can still be comfortable on the shady south side of the Valley. The first snowfall of the season usually comes to Yosemite sometime after November 15th; the last snows fall sometime before April 15. Only during the dead of winter will the snow remain unmelted in the shade. Winter climbing activity is usually slow, although there can be long periods of clear, dry, and mild weather.

The main information office for Yosemite National Park can be reached at P.O Box 577, Yosemite, California 95389, or by calling (209)372-0264 for a recording, or (209)372-0265 during business hours. A road, weather, and camping recording is available at (209)372-0209. The Public Information office can be reached at (209)372-0529 for current information on peregrine falcon closures and other climbing concerns.

Staying in the Park

An entrance fee must be paid upon entering the park, which can be dealt with in one of three ways. Visitors can purchase a $5 per car one-week pass; a $15 Yosemite Pass, which allows yearly access to Yosemite only; or a $25 Golden Eagle Pass, which allows annual passage into national parks and monuments throughout the country. During the summer season, from June 1 to September 15, there is a seven-day camping limit in the valley. There is a 30-day limit the rest of the year.

The National Park Service is the governing authority within Yosemite, and the park service's obligation is the preservation of this national resource. Thus, the service is responsible for law enforcement, ambulance service, roads, campgrounds (although the reservation system is handled by Mistix), water, sewage, trash, etc. It also conducts search and rescue operations when necessary. Also, not to be eclipsed by the above-mentioned, the park service handles resource management and interpretive programs.

The concessionaire in Yosemite offers and operates virtually all of the goods and services within the park. The medical clinic, Ansel Adams Studio and an automatic teller machine are a few exceptions. A general store, post office, medical clinic, visitor center, garage and delicatessen are located in Yosemite Village. Curry Village, Yosemite Lodge and Ahwahnee Hotel provide accommodations ranging from modest tent-cabins to fairly luxurious hotel rooms. Additional public facilities can be found at these locations as well. At Yosemite Lodge, for instance, there is a year-round cafeteria, restaurant, bar and gift shop/convenience store. Of special interest are the showers at Curry Village ($1.25, soap and towel provided). Also at Curry Village, there is a mountain shop, the Yosemite Mountaineering School and Guide Service, and the usual cafeteria, convenience store, fast food, etc. The laundromat can be found at Curry Housekeeping Camp. The only gas station in the valley is adjacent to Sunnyside Campground.

Six campgrounds are located in the valley. Sunnyside Campground (also know as Camp Four) is the place with the most atmosphere, and is the popular choice among climbers. In this boulder-strewn walk-in campground, individuals are charged $2 per night for shared sites, with up to six people allowed in each site. It can be overflowing or deserted, depending on the time of year and weather conditions. Most of the other campgrounds provide conventional car camping, with sites going for $15 per night with a six-person, two-car maximum. Advance reservations for car camping are necessary from spring to mid-fall, particularly on weekends. Reservations may be made up to, but no more than, eight weeks in advance of your visit by calling Destinet toll-free at (800)436-7275. From outside the US, call Destinet at (619)452-8787. Mindful of the great demand for campsites in Yosemite Valley, callers are advised that the phone numbers become operational starting at 7:00 am Pacific Standard Time. Reservations by mail can be made up to five months in advance, starting on the 15th of each month. The mailing address for Destinet is 9450 Carroll Park Drive, San Diego, California 92121. Reservations may also be made in person at the campground Reservation Office in Curry Village. Pets are permitted in Upper Pines designated campgrounds only, and must be leashed at all times. Pets are not allowed on any park trails.

A free shuttle bus system runs between the lodge, Village, Ahwahnee and Curry, which provides easy access to climbs within the east end of the valley. Bicycles work well in the main valley but for climbers without cars, arranging rides with other climbers may be necessary to get to cliffs in the lower canyon.

Suggestions and Precautions

For the climber interested in bouldering, an excellent bouldering circuit extends from the western end of Camp Four east to Swan Slab. Other prime bouldering spots are the start of the Four Mile Trail, below Sentinel Rock, and near the Curry Housekeeping Camp.

Poison oak is found throughout the valley, although it grows most abundantly west of the Pohono Bridge, and throughout the Lower Merced Canyon. Rattlesnakes may be encountered in warm weather months basking in the sun along the base of cliffs. Rarely do they provide more than just a notable nuisance on an approach to a climb.

Yosemite Valley is no wilderness, and the climber must share the relatively small space with thousands of other visitors. It is still possible for the imaginative climber to find a quiet day, alone with the cliffs and the swallows. While the crowded camping experience may leave some climbers cold, those who complain of the crowded climbing experience are simply unimaginative in their route finding abilities. Nighttime is a different story; Yosemite after dark is known among the regulars for its boring nights as much as its exciting days.The options are limited; the Lodge-wandering circuit with bar or restaurant, or back to camp. Books help, but it's difficult to find a place to read. Solution? — There is no solution, but you will have lots of company.

Yosemite Valley has all the ingredients of a small town, and does not revolve around the world of the climber. About 1,200 people live or work throughout the year in the park, mostly in Yosemite Valley; the number rises to perhaps 2,200 during the height of the tourist season. These residents all fall into various social groups but, except for a minute percentage, share a total lack of interest in climbing or climbers. Curry employees, both career professionals and the incredibly temporary juveniles, form the bulk of the work force. Then there is the Park Service employee, from the dedicated naturalist to the Law Enforcement Officer. It is the latter group that spells trouble for anyone who loves to climb a lot in Yosemite and also needs to be loud about it. Keeping in mind that to most of the residents of Yosemite, climbers are merely tourists who spend little, can be disorderly, and try to stay as long as possible, it is not difficult to understand why some Law Enforcement rangers see their job as challenged by those who bend the rules. There are rangers who climb very actively, however, and keeping in mind that the mandate of the Park Service is to protect the natural resource, most rangers will be found to be very helpful.

Interaction between the Park Service and the climbing community is bridged in one other way; with a couple of sites in Camp Four reserved for the free use of the most experienced Yosemite climbers, the Park has a competent and obligated source for paid help on technical searches and rescues. The experience of the Yosemite Search and Rescue Team is invaluable to all climbers by providing insight on the prevention of major accidents.

ENVIRONMENTAL ISSUES:
The National Park Service Perspective

The National Park Service was created in 1916 to "provide for the enjoyment of the visitor" and to "leave the park unimpaired for future generations." Unfortunately, these two goals often conflict, and balancing the immediate demands of visitors with the long-term health of the park is a task that often generates controversy. Climbers and non-climbers alike effect, and are affected by, Park Service land use policy.

Climbing is one of the oldest recreational uses in Yosemite, predating the establishment of the park in 1890. James Hutchings, John Muir, and Clarence King had little impact on the mountains they climbed, using no equipment that marred the rock and leaving nothing behind. With the exception of George Anderson's bolt route on the Northeast Face of Half Dome in 1875, this benign relationship prevailed until the 1930s, when the use of pitons, bolts, and other modern climbing methods became popular. Increasing numbers of climbers through the 1940s, '50s, and '60s led to noticeable rock damage and the clean climbing revolution of the '70s.

Given the large number of climbers and the nature of the damage they cause, the Park Service has enacted surprisingly little regulation of the sport. This is partly due to the historic use of the park for climbing and partly because climbers have traditionally policed themselves. Indeed, for many years climbing and environmentalism were seen as close partners until recently; the "Sierra Club Bulletin" published climbing stories and route descriptions next to articles on preserving wilderness areas. Many of the outstanding conservationists in American history were climbers, notably Muir and David Brower. To Muir, the term "mountaineer" implied that one not only climbed and felt at home in the high country, but loved and cared for mountains as well.

This perception, however, has changed. Climbing is now seen by some people as just one more destructive use of the land. In several areas of the country, both private landowners and public land agencies have responded to climber-caused environmental damage by restricting climbing. The list of problems caused by climbers is lengthy: multiple approach trails and the subsequent erosion, disturbance of cliff dwelling animals, destruction of American Indian rock art, litter, chalk marks, pin scars, bolts, chopped holds and aid placements, glued-on artificial holds, gardening (an ironic euphemism for destroying vegetation), "trails" of lichen-free rock that can be seen from miles away, bivy ledges that reek of urine and feces, chopping down trees close to a route, bright-colored rappel slings, etc. Virtually all of these impacts have occurred in Yosemite in the last few years. Some of these impacts are reversible (litter, feces, chalk) while some are permanent (bolts, chopped holds, pin scars).

No other users of the park are permitted to cause such damage. These practices not only degrade the natural environment and diminish the climbing experience, but are also noticed by the non-climbing public. The average visitor to Yosemite expects to view the park's famous cliffs without seeing chalk marks, bolts, and rappel slings. Visitor complaints (from non-climbers and climbers) about this damage are common.

Look around you when you go climbing; is erosion turning that approach trail into a gully? Is there a maze of trails where one would do? Is your climbing route visible from across the valley as a white path up the lichen-covered rock? Note the absence of small trees, bushes and flowering plants that were there a few years ago. None of that will regrow overnight. (Soil formation and lichen growth can take hundreds of years.) Now extend the damage you've identified ahead a decade, a generation, or several generations. What will it look like then? (How many new routes will have gone up in that time?) Compare that future with what you think the park should look like. For how long do you think the park should be maintained in its natural state? Do your wishes match the changes you see around you?

Clearly, some limitations are necessary. Currently, motorized drilling, cutting trees, attaching artificial holds, and littering are illegal in the park. If present trends continue, more control of climbing activity may be required to protect the natural environment. If climbers undertake reforms themselves, additional regulations may not be necessary.

What can you do to protect the environment while preserving your climbing freedom? First, climb in an environmentally responsible manner. Minimize your impact. Follow the "Climber's Code" recently published by the Access Fund. Second, get involved. Write the park superintendent (NPS, PO Box 577, Yosemite, CA 95389) and express your opinions on climbing issues. Contact the Access Fund (PO Box 17010, Boulder, Colorado 80308) and local climbing groups. Third, exercise restraint. Just because a route can be climbed doesn't mean it should be climbed. Does El Cap really need another route with pitch after pitch of chiselled copperhead placements? Is it worth destroying hundreds of square feet of cliffside vegetation for yet another 5.11 face climb? Is it worth incurring public complaints by putting up another bolted route in Lower Falls amphitheater? Is it really necessary to place bolts up a route that can be easily top-roped? Only by seriously considering such questions can Yosemite's walls and your freedom be preserved.

Ethics and Code of Conduct

Several climber-use issues have come to a turning point. More people coupled with resource-impacting trends on and around the walls of Yosemite have brought a call for a deeper understanding of why National Parks, particularly Yosemite, stand out as special. Practices which, in the past, have been technically illegal or at least counter to the spirit and resources of Yosemite, have often been ignored. Rules and regulations flourish where common sense and self-control are absent, and rock police are not the real answer anyway. Literally and figuratively many paths cross in the pursuit of the wild spirit and freedom inherent to Yosemite climbing. Ironically, awareness, accountability, and self-restraint will preserve it.

The enlightening National Park Service perspective preceeded this, however here are a few highlighted issues wall climbers need to be aware of:

- Stay current with issues and regulations (peregrine falcon closures, etc.)
- Climb in a safe and responsible manner. Rescue helicopters in a meadow and an army of rescuers on the summit make for big time environmental impact.
- Use established approach/descent trails when possible.
- Above 4,200 feet is designated wilderness. This includes all the wall routes of Yosemite.
- Camping at the base is considered out-of-bounds camping and is illegal.
- Park Service considers equipment abandoned after 24 hours. Fixed ropes and "high-point" gear caches are high profile.
- Don't throw haul bags or anything else off cliffs.
- Don't litter. Pack all trash out.
- Dispose of human waste properly. Contain it. A PVC 'pipe-bomb' or other bombproof containers will help keep routes and bivy spots from being 'gross-out health hazards.' Ejecting garbage and waste, then returning to the base to pick-up is not a real solution. With continuous ascents almost always in progress (especially El Capitan), deposit of dumpage at the base is unacceptable. A sanitary dump station is located at Upper Pines Campground. No plastic, please.
- Car pool or ride a bicycle when possible. Cutting down on overnight parking at El Capitan would be particularly helpful.

Thanks for taking the time to read this, thereby moving a step closer to a solution.

Yo Dude!

In case we didn't make it clear enough—To those of you who litter, trash vegetation, cut your own trail, don't pack out your shit, chisel and chip: YOU'RE A JERK. You have no business being on the mountain, giving a bad name to the rest of the climbers. Sell your gear and quit. We don't want your kind, no matter what you can climb.

STAYING ALIVE
John Dill, NPS Search and Rescue

Most climbers do a good job coping with the hazards of their sport, yet more than 100 climbing accidents occur in the park every year. What factors contribute to them? What, if anything, can climbers do to avoid them? And just how dangerous is climbing, anyway? With these questions in mind, the National Park Service (NPS) recently examined most of the serious accidents that occurred in the park during the years from 1970 through 1990. The conclusions provide interesting reading for those wishing to stay alive.

Fifty-one climbers died from traumatic injuries in that period. A dozen more, critically hurt, would have died without rapid transport and medical treatment. In addition, there were many serious but survivable injuries, from fractured skulls to broken legs (at least 50 fractures per year), and a much larger number of cuts, bruises, and sprains.

Not surprisingly, most injuries occurred during leader falls and involved feet, ankles, or lower legs; for many, these are the accepted risks of climbing. However, leader falls accounted for only 25% of the fatal and near-fatal traumatic injuries; roughly 10% were from rockfall, 25% from being deliberately unroped, and 40% from simple mistakes with gear. Many cases are not clear cut; several factors may share the credit, and it is sometimes hard to quantify the weird adventures climbers have.

Not to be overlooked in the body count are environmental injuries. Inadequately equipped for the weather, four climbers died of hypothermia and perhaps 45 more would have died of the cold or the heat if not rescued.

Fifteen to 25 parties require an NPS rescue each year. Sixty more climbers stagger into Yosemite's medical clinic on their own, and an unknown number escape statistical immortality by seeking treatment outside the park (or at the Mountain Room Bar).

Most Yosemite victims are experienced climbers: 60% have been climbing for three years or more, lead at least 5.10, are in good condition, and climb frequently. Short climbs and big walls, easy routes and desperate ones — all get their share of the accidents.

The NPS keeps no statistics on how many climbers use the park, but 25,000 to 50,000 climber-days annually is a fair estimate. With this in mind, 2.5 deaths and a few serious injuries per year may seem a pretty low rate. It's much too high, however, if your climbing career is cut short by a broken hip, or worse. It's also too high when you consider that at least 80% of the fatalities, and many injuries, were easily preventable. In case after case, ignorance, a casual attitude, and/or some form of distraction proved to be the most dangerous aspects of the sport.

As the saying goes, "good judgement comes from bad experience." In the pages that follow are condensed 21 years of bad experience — the situations Yosemite climbers faced, the mistakes they made, and some recommendations for avoiding bad experiences of your own. This information comes in many cases from the victims' own analysis or from those of their peers.

Environmental Dangers

On Oct. 11, 1983, a climber on El Cap collapsed from heat exhaustion. On Oct. 11, 1984, a party on Washington Column was immobilized by hypothermia. You can expect this range of weather year-round.

Heat No Yosemite climber has died from the heat, but a half-dozen parties have come close. Too exhausted to move, they survived only because death by drying-up is a relatively slow process, allowing rescuers time to get there.

Temperatures on the sunny walls often exceed 100°f, but even in cool weather, climbing all day requires lots of water. The generally accepted minimum, two quarts per person per day, is just that — a minimum. It may not replace what you use, so don't let the desire for a light haulbag be your overriding concern, and take extra for unanticipated delays. Do not put all your water in a single container, and watch out for leaks.

If you find yourself rationing water, remember that dehydration will seriously sap your strength, slowing you even further. It's not uncommon to go from mere thirst to a complete standstill in a single day. Continuing up may be the right choice but several climbers have said, "I should have gone down while I could."

Storms We still hear climbers say, "It never rains in Yosemite." In fact, there are serious storms year-round. Four climbers have died of hypothermia and almost 50 have been rescued, most of whom would not have survived otherwise. Several were very experienced, with winter alpine routes, Yosemite walls, and stormy bivouacs to their credit — experts, by most measures. In many cases they took sub-standard gear, added another mistake or two, and couldn't deal with the water.

Mountain thunderstorms are common in spring, summer, and fall. They may appear suddenly out of a clear blue sky and rapidly shift position, their approach concealed by the route you are on. A few minutes warning may be all that you get. Thunderstorms may last only a couple of hours, but they are very intense, with huge amounts of near-freezing water often mixed with hail, strong winds, and lightning. The runoff can be a foot deep and fast enough to cause rockfall. A common result is a panicky retreat, a jammed rope, and cries for help. (The standard joke is that someone will drown on a Tuolumne climb one of these days. It's actually possible.)

No climber has died in such a storm yet because rescuers were able to respond. No climbers have died from lightning either, but there have been several near misses, and hikers on Half Dome and elsewhere have been killed. Get out of the way of a thunderstorm as fast as you can, and avoid summits and projections.

The big Pacific storm systems have proven more dangerous. They sweep through the Sierra at any time of year, most frequently from September through May. They are unpredictable, often appearing back-to-back after several weeks of gorgeous, mind-numbing weather. It may rain on Half Dome in January and snow there in July. These storms are dangerous because they are usually warm enough to be wet, even in winter, yet always cold enough to kill an unprotected climber. They last from one to several days, offering little respite if you can't escape.

With no soil to absorb it, rain on the walls quickly collects into streams and waterfalls, pouring off overhangs and down the corner you're trying to climb up or sleep in. Wind blows the water in all directions, including straight up. It may rip apart a plastic tube tent or blow a portaledge up and down until the tubing breaks or the fly rips. Overhanging faces and other "sheltered" spots are not always immune — rain and waterfalls several yards away may be blown directly onto your bivy, and runoff will wick down your anchor rope. Even a slow but steady leak into your shelter can defeat you. Temperatures may drop, freezing solid the next pitch, your ropes, and your wet sleeping bag.

Once cold and wet, you are in real trouble and your options run out. If you leave your shelter to climb or rappel, you deteriorate more rapidly from the wind and water. Even with good gear, water runs down your sleeve every time you reach up. As your body temperature drops, you begin making dumb mistakes, such as clipping in wrong or dropping your rack. You are seriously hypothermic, and soon you will just hang there, no longer caring. It happens quickly. In two separate incidents, climbers on the last pitch of The Nose left what protection they had to make a run for the top. They all died on that pitch.

Staying put may be no better. If you need help, no one may see you or hear you, and reaching you may take days longer than in good weather. Survivors say they had no idea how helpless they'd be until it happened to them. To find out for yourself, stand in the spray of a garden hose on a cold, windy night. How long will you last?

Big Wall Bivouacs

Despite this grim scenario, reasonable precautions will turn stormy big-wall bivouacs into mere annoyances:

- Check the forecast just before you start up but don't rely on it. For several parties it provided no warning whatsoever.
- Assume you'll be hit by a storm, and that you'll not have a choice of bivies.
- Ask friends to check on you if the weather or the forecast turns bad.
- Evaluate ahead of time the problems of retreat from any point on the route. Did you bring a bolt kit? How about a "cheater stick" for clipping into bolt hangers and stuffing cams into out-of-reach cracks as you flee down an overhanging pitch?
- If it's starting to rain, think twice about climbing "just one more pitch" — once wet you won't dry out. It's better to set up your bivy while you're still dry.
- Frozen ropes are useless for climbing or retreating, as several parties found out. Put them away early.

All such hints and tricks aside, the bottom line is your ability to sit out the storm. Your first priority is to keep the wind and outside water away. Second is to be insulated enough to stay warm, even though you are wet from your own condensation.

- Stick with high quality gear in good condition, and don't leave key items behind to ease the hauling. Don't go up with a poorly equipped partner; it will be your neck as well.
- For insulation, never rely on cotton or down (even if it's covered with one of the waterproof/breathable fabrics). Even nylon absorbs water.

Wool, polypropylene, and polyester insulators stay relatively warm when wet, and the synthetics dry fastest. Take along long underwear, warm pants, sweater, jacket, balaclava/hat, gloves, sleeping bag, insulating pad, extra socks or booties, and plenty of food and water—dehydration hastens hypothermia.

- For rain, use coated nylon, sailors' oilskins, or the waterproof/breathable fabrics. Take rain pants and jacket, overmitts, bivy bag, and hammock or portaledge with waterproof fly. The fly is critical — it must overlap your hammock generously and be of heavy material, in excellent condition, with strong, well-sealed seams. For sleeping on ledges, take a big tent fly or a piece of heavy-duty, reinforced plastic and the means to pitch it. Then hope that your ledge doesn't turn into a lake. Do you know how to run your anchor through the fly without making a hole? Did you spend more for lycra than rainwear?

- **WARNING:** Several climbers have blamed the waterproof/breathable fabrics for their close calls. They claim that no version of it can take the punishment of a storm on the walls. Whether true or not, you must be the judge; test all of your gear ahead of time under miserable conditions, but where your exit is an easy one.

For more information on bad weather, including a description of the waterproof anchor, see "Surviving Big Walls," by Brian Bennett, *Climbing*, Feb./Mar. 1990.

Unplanned Bivouacs Getting caught by darkness is common, especially on the longer one-day climbs and descent routes, e.g., Royal Arches and Cathedral Rocks. It happens easily — a late start, a slow partner, off route, a jammed or dropped rope, or a sprained ankle. Usually it's nothing to get upset about, but if you are unprepared, even a cold wind or a mild storm becomes serious. One death and several close calls occurred this way. To avoid becoming a statistic:

- Consider the following gear for each person's day pack: long underwear, gloves, balaclava, rain jacket and pants (which double as wind protection). In warmer weather, all can be of the lightweight variety. If that's too heavy for you, at least take one of those disposable plastic rainsuits or tube tents that occupy virtually no space. Take more warm clothes in colder weather. A headlamp with spare bulb and new batteries is very important for finding safe anchors, signaling for help, or avoiding that bivy altogether. Matches and heat-tabs will light wet wood. Food and water increase your safety after a night of shivering.

- Keep your survival gear with you whenever practical, not with your partner — climbers get separated from their gear, and each other, in imaginative ways, sometimes with serious consequences.

- Standing in slings on poor anchors is not the way to spend a night. If a bivy is inevitable, don't climb until the last moment; find a safe, sheltered, and/or comfortable spot while you've got enough light.

Descents Consult the guidebook and your friends, but be wary of advice that the way down is obvious; look the route over ahead of time. If you carry a topo of the way up, consider one for the way down, or a photograph. Your ultimate protection is route-finding ability, and that takes experience. Some trouble spots: North Dome Gully, the Kat Walk, Michael's Ledge.

- Many rappel epics are born when an easy descent, often a walk-off, is missed. Search for it thoroughly before you commit to a big drop — it may be well worth the effort.
- Conversely, footprints and rappel anchors often lead nowhere — they were someone else's mistake. Be willing and able to retrace your steps and remember that the crux may not be at the top.
- To further evaluate an uncertain descent, consider rappelling a single line as far as possible (160 feet if one rope, 320 feet if two). Learn to be comfortable on the rope and be willing to swing around a corner to look for the next anchor. Carry enough gear to go back up your rope and know how to use it.
- Any time you can't see anchors all the way to the ground, take the gear to set your own. That includes established descents, since ice and rockfall frequently destroy anchors. It sometimes means carrying a bolt kit.
- Consider taking a second (7-9mm) rope, even for one-rope descents and walk-offs. You'll save time, depend on fewer anchors, leave less gear, and more easily reverse the climbing route in an emergency. This is one advantage of leading on double ropes. But don't forget that thinner ropes are more vulnerable to sharp edges.
- Friction from wet or twisted ropes, slings, ledges, cracks and flakes may jam your rope. Plan ahead when you rig the anchor and be willing to leave gear behind to avoid friction. You can retrieve the gear tomorrow.
- Rappelling through trees? Consider short rappels, from tree to tree. It's slow but avoids irretrievable snarls.
- Is your rope jammed? You can go back up and rerig if you still have both ends, so keep them until you're sure it will pull or you have to let go. If you do have to climb that rope, be careful that it isn't jammed by a sharp edge. Don't forget to untie the knots in the ends before you pull.
- Dropped ropes and gear can be more than just embarrassing; without a rescue, a stranded climber is a dead climber, even in good weather. When transferring gear, clip it to its next anchor before unclipping it from the current one.

Loose Rock There's plenty of it in Yosemite. Ten percent of all injuries are associated with rockfall, including six deaths and one permanent disability. In several other deaths, loose rock was implicated but not confirmed, e.g., possible broken handholds and failed placements. Spontaneous rockfall is not the problem — all the fatal and serious accidents were triggered by the victim, the rope, or by climbers above.

Rocks lying on ledges and in steep gullies are obviously dangerous. Not so obvious is that old reliable mantle block, five times your weight, wedged in place, and worn smooth by previous climbers. Yet with distressing regularity, "bombproof" blocks, flakes, and even ledges collapse under body weight, spit out cams, or fracture from the pressure of a piton. The forces placed on anchors and protection, even from rappelling, may be far higher than you generate in a test. Handholds may pass your scrutiny, then fail in mid-move. The rock you pull off can break your leg after falling only a couple of feet. Finally, watch out for rotten rock, responsible for at least two of these fatalities. It's common on the last couple of pitches of climbs that go to the rim of the Valley, e.g., Yosemite Point Buttress and Washington Column.

The East Buttress of Middle Cathedral Rock is a well-known bowling alley, the site of many rockfall injuries. The Northwest Face of Half Dome is another, with the added excitement of tourist "firing squads" on the summit. But the most dangerous, surprisingly, may be El Cap; on rock so steep, loose blocks balance precariously and big flakes wait for an unlucky hand to trigger the final fracture.

Some rockfall accidents may not be preventable, short of staying home, but being alert to the hazard and following a few guidelines will cut the injury rate:

- Consider a helmet for loose routes. (See "Helmets," page 17.)
- Throw in an occasional piece on long, easy runouts, as insurance against the unpredictability of the medium.
- Avoid rotten rock as protection, even if you can back it up. When it fails it endangers everyone below.
- Ropes launch almost as many missiles as climbers do. Watch where you run your lead rope. Use directionals to keep it away from loose — and sharp — stuff, and check it frequently. Keep in mind that your bag or pack, when hauled, may dislodge everything in its path. When you pull your rappel ropes, stand to one side, look up, and watch out for delayed rockfall.
- You have no control over a party above you, and by being below you accept the risk. If you are catching up, don't crowd them — ask for permission to pass. You can probably get by them safely, but remember that climbers have been killed or hurt by rocks dislodged by parties above, including those they allowed to pass. The party you want to pass may have gotten an early start to avoid that risk, and they have no obligation to let you by. When you are above someone else, including your partner, put yourself in their shoes. Slow down, watch your feet and the rope.

Climbing Unroped

Everybody does it, to some extent. There's no reason to stop, but good reason to be cautious: fourteen climbers were killed and two critically injured while deliberately unroped. At least eight climbed 5.10 or better. Most, if not all, of those accidents were avoidable. You may find yourself unroped in several situations — on third-class terrain, spontaneously on fifth-class, and while deliberately free-soloing a route.

Third class terrain may be easy, but add a bit of sand, loose or wet rock, darkness, plus a moment of distraction, and the rating becomes meaningless. Four climbers have died this way, typically on approach and descent routes such as North Dome Gully, all in spots that did not demand a rope.

Sometimes you lose the way on the approach, or unrope at what you thought was the top of the climb, only to find a few feet of "easy" fifth-class blocking your way. Your rope is tucked away in your pack, and you're in a hurry. Before you go on, remember that you didn't plan to free-solo an unknown quantity today. Four died this way, falling from fifth-class terrain that they were climbing on the spur of the moment.

Seven of the 14 killed were rappelling or otherwise tied in. They unroped while still on fifth-class rock, for various reasons of convenience, without clipping into a nearby anchor. Three slipped off their stances, a ledge collapsed under another, one decided to down-climb the last few feet, and two tried to climb their rappel ropes hand-over-hand to attend to some problem. Like the previous group, they all went unroped onto fifth class terrain on the spur of the moment. In addition, they all had a belay immediately available. Did its nearness give them a false sense of security?

No true free-soloer has been killed yet, although one, critically hurt, survived only by the speed of his rescue. A death will happen eventually, possibly the result of a loose hold. Is the free-soloer more alert to the task, having planned it in advance, than those who unroped on the spur of the moment? Were the unlucky fourteen still relaxed in their minds, not quite attuned to their new situation? We can only speculate.

Keep these cases and the hidden hazards in mind as you travel through any steep terrain. Be aware of what is under foot, and in hand, at each moment. Be patient enough to retrace your steps to find the easy way, and if there's a belay hanging in front of you, think twice before rejecting it. Finally, remember that your climbing ability has probably been measured on clean, rated routes, not on unpredictable sand and wet moss. Being a 5.11 climber does not mean you can fly.

Leading

Nine climbers died and six were critically injured in leader- fall accidents involving inadequate protection. Most fell simply because the moves were hard, and several were victims of broken holds. They were all injured because they hit something before their protection stopped them. Either they did not place enough protection (one-third of the cases) or it failed under the force of the fall (the remaining two-thirds). In every case, their injuries were serious because they fell headfirst or on their sides — the head, neck, or trunk took a lethal blow. Half fell 50 feet or less, the climber falling the shortest distance (25 feet) died, and the longest (270 feet!) survived.

Were these catastrophes avoidable? It's sometimes hard to tell, but the answer is often yes. Here are a few lessons frequently learned the hard way:

- Climbers frequently describe the belaying habits they see on Yosemite routes as "frightening." Before you start up, how frightening is your belay? Can the anchor withstand pulls in all directions? Is there more than one piece, with the load shared? Is the tie-in snug and in line with the fall force? Is your belayer experienced with that belay gadget and in position to operate it effectively when you fall? (You'd be surprised.) Will you clip through a bombproof directional as you start up, even on an easy pitch?

- Don't cheat on your ground fall calculations. (A good belayer will keep you honest.) With rope stretch and slack in the system, you may fall twice as far below your last protection as you are above it — if it holds.

- Nuts want to fall out. One that self-cleans below you may turn a comfortable lead into a ground-fall situation. Or, during a fall, the top piece may hold just long enough for the rope to yank the lower nuts out sideways, and then also fail. For more reliable placements, set those nuts with a tug and sling them generously. A tug on a marginal nut, however, is worthless as a test. Tiny nubbins may hold it firmly under those conditions but give way in a fall. Be especially cautious about placements you can't see. Back them up.

- Camming devices "fail" regularly, but it's seldom the fault of the device. It's more likely due to haste, coupled with undeserved faith in technology. As with nuts, a blind placement — often in a layback crack — may feel solid but be worthless.

- Fixed pitons loosen from freeze-thaw cycles and repeated use. They may not have been installed well to begin with. A hammer is the only reliable way to test and reset them, but you don't see many hammers on free routes these days. You don't see them on rappel routes, either, but you may find yourself hanging from anchors that belong in a museum. If you don't test pitons properly, do not depend on them — routinely back them up.

- There is no reliable way to test bolts but plenty of reasons to want to. For example, the common ¼" split-shaft type was not designed or intended for life support, let alone for rock climbing. Their quality varies; several have broken under body weight, and others like them await you. Reliability also depends on the quality of the rock and the skill of the bolter. Add years of weathering and mistreatment by climbers and the result is many bolts that are easily pulled out by fingers or a sharp yank with a sling. Several bolt hangers have cracked as well, with one fatal accident so far.

- Never test a bolt with a hammer. Instead, examine the surrounding rock, the bolt, and the hanger for cracks, and hope they are large enough to see. Is the bolt tight and fully seated in the hole? Is the nut snug? Good luck.

- Back up all untested fixed protection.

- Okay. So you know this stuff. You're a little shaky on the lead right now and you've had some trouble getting your pro to stick, but the book said this was 5.10a, and besides, two teenage girls just walked up this pitch. It's only 20 feet more and one of those pieces is bound to hold. Think for a minute. Are you willing to free-solo this pitch? Keep your answer in mind as you climb, because poorly placed protection amounts to just that — you may not be deliberately unroped, but you might as well be.

About Falling There's an art to falling safely — like a cat. Bouldering helps build the alertness required. Controlling your fall may be out of the question on those 200-foot screamers, but it will reduce the risk of injury from routine falls. Whenever possible, land on your feet — even if you break your leg, absorbing the shock this way may save your life. Laybacks and underclings hold special risks in this regard — you are already leaning back, and if you lose your grip the friction of your feet on the rock may rotate you into a headfirst — and backward — dive.

- A chest harness will not keep you from tumbling as you free-fall, but it will turn you upright as the rope comes tight. This reduces the chance of serious injury during the braking phase and may be life-saving if you hang there for long, already seriously hurt.

- The wall may look vertical below you, but even glancing off a steep slab can be fatal. Three climbers died this way.
- Pendulum falls are particularly dangerous. If you swing into a corner from 20 feet to one side of your protection, you will hit with the same bone-breaking speed as when striking a ledge in a 20- foot vertical fall. The crucial difference is, you are "landing" on your side, exposing vital organs to the impact. Two climbers died this way and others suffered serious injuries. Even small projections are dangerous: a 20-foot swing on Glacier Point Apron fractured a skull, and another smashed a pelvis. In a pendulum there is no difference between a leader and a follower fall; don't forget to protect your second from this fate as you lead a hard traverse.

Learning to Lead Four of the 15 killed or critically injured in leader falls were good climbers on well-defined routes, but the majority were intermediates, often off-route. There may be a couple of lessons in that.

- Don't get cocky because you just led your first 5.8 or your protection held on your first fall. Experienced climbers have died from errors "only a beginner would make," so you have plenty of time left in your career to screw up.
- Climbing and protecting are separate skills but both keep you alive. Don't challenge yourself in both at the same time — you may not have the skill and presence of mind to get out of a tight spot. If you're out to push your limits, pick a route that's well defined and easy to protect, place extra pieces for practice, and be willing and equipped to back off.
- Route finding is another survival skill. A mistake here can quickly put you over your head in climbing, protecting, or both. Learn to look ahead and recognize what you want to avoid. Climb it mentally before you climb it physically.
- Some "easy" terrain in the valley is actually pretty dangerous. Low-angle gullies are often full of loose blocks cemented together with moss. Opportunities for protection may be scarce and route finding subtle. These are not usually cataloged routes. Three or four climbers have been killed, or nearly so, on such terrain while looking for easy routes to climb.
- **A Leading Problem:** The last pitch of The Nutcracker provides a subtle challenge for the fledgling 5.8 leader. Once over the mantle, you may relax as you contemplate the easy climb to the top. But if you forget about your protection, a slip in the next few moves may send you back over the side to crash into the slab below. This pitch has scored several broken ankles when the fall was longer than expected, and a more serious injury is possible. There are many such situations in the Valley, and one key to safety is to look below you while you plan ahead.

The Belay Chain

Whether you are climbing, rappelling, or just sitting on a ledge, the belay chain is what connects you to the rock. There are many links, and mistakes with almost every one have killed 22 climbers, 40% of all Yosemite climbing fatalities. In every case the cause was human error. In every case the death was completely preventable, not by the subtle skills of placing protection on the lead, but by some simple precaution to keep the belay chain intact. Experienced climbers outnumbered the inexperienced in this category, two to one.

Mistakes with the belay chain can occur at any time. Make one and you'll fall to the end of the rope . . . or farther. Minor injuries are rare. Here are some key points to remember:

- Before you commit yourself to a system, always apply a few pounds of tension in the directions in which it will be loaded, analyzing it like an engineer — what if this happens . . . or that? Check every link, from the buckle of your harness to the rock around your anchor. You would be amazed at the inadequate systems often used by experienced climbers, even though it takes only a few seconds to run a proper check.

- Both lives depend on that system, so go through it with your partner. Nine climbers have died in multi-victim accidents.

- Check the system periodically while you're using it. Forces may change direction (two died when their anchors failed for this reason), ropes and slings can wear through (serious injuries and one death) and gear can come undone (two died when a wiggling bolt hanger unscrewed its nut — they were relying on a single bolt.)

- Are you about to rappel? Stay clipped to the anchor for a few seconds. Check both the anchor and your brake system, as above. If one anchor point fails, will you remain attached to others? Are the knots in your rappel slings secure? Did you check every inch of those fixed slings for damage? Skipping these precautions cost eight lives plus serious injuries, from poorly tied slings, partially dismantled anchors (a simple misunderstanding), relying on single carabiners, and other reasons. The next accident may be caused by something new, but it will have been preventable by double-checking.

- Two climbers died by rappelling off the ends of their ropes, even though both had tied knots in the ends as a safety measure. In one case the knots pulled through the brake. In the second, the victim forgot to double-check the ropes after a knot had been untied to deal with a problem. Knots are still a recommended safety procedure, but do not take anything for granted. Tie both strands into one knot or knot each separately — there are pros and cons to each method.

- When rappelling in unpredictable circumstances — dark, windy, poor communications, unknown anchors below — consider a Prusik Hitch or a mechanical ascender as a safety. If improperly handled, neither one may stop you if you fall — they are primarily for quickly but deliberately stopping yourself to deal with other emergencies. Both of those who rappelled off their ropes would have survived with safeties.

- In separate incidents, five climbers somehow became detached from their ropes while climbing with mechanical ascenders — not the fault of the devices. Only three were tied to their ropes at all, at the lower end. All five died because they had not tied in "short," leaving themselves open to a long fall. To tie in short, tie a loop in the rope a few feet below your ascenders and clip it to your harness. As you climb, repeat the process often enough to limit your fall should you come off your rope. At the very least, do this when you must pass one ascender around protection, traverse (three deaths), or change to another rope. (Is that other rope anchored well? One climber died, partly because his wasn't. Ask your partner first.) In addition, always be tied into both of your ascenders.

- Self-belayers should also tie in short — one died when his Prusik belay melted during a fall (a Prusik cord too large for the rope). At least two were treated to close calls when other types of self-belay systems jammed open.

- Clip into a new belay point before unclipping from the old one. During those few, vulnerable seconds, pitons have pulled, hero loops have broken, rocks have struck, and feet have slipped.

- Three climbers were killed and one critically injured by "failures" of single-carabiner tie-ins and rappel anchors. Be careful of relying on a single non-locking carabiner for any link in the chain. The rope or sling may flip over the gate and unclip itself, especially if it is slack, or shock-loaded. Even if you watch it carefully and/or it is "safely" under tension, you may become distracted. One climber died when his Figure Eight descender unclipped while he was busy passing a knot on rappel. (He should have tied in short.) For those critical points, use either two non-locking carabiners with gates opposed and reversed, or a locking carabiner. Don't forget to lock it! For many applications the two-carabiner method is safer and faster to operate.

- Ropes have been cut in three fatal accidents. They did not break, but were stressed over sharp edges, a condition never intended by the manufacturer. Two of these accidents were avoidable: one climber should have tied in short to prevent a 100 foot fall that cut the rope; the other should have protected a fixed rope from a well-defined sharp edge. Ascending a rope produces a weighted, see-sawing action that can destroy it, even over a rounded, moderately rough, edge.

- As with ropes, most gear failure falls into the misuse category. Failure from a design or manufacturing flaw is rare. It was the initiating factor in one fatal accident — three climbers died when a bolt hanger broke at a two-bolt rappel anchor. The tragic outcome would have been avoided, however, had the climbers noticed they were not properly backed up to the second bolt.

These cases illustrate one of the rules most commonly overlooked: BACK YOURSELF UP. No matter what initially pulled, broke, slipped, jammed, or cut, the incident became an accident because the climber did not carefully ask himself, "What if. . . ?" By leaving yourself open, you are betting against a variety of unpredictable events. You don't lose very often, but when you do, you may lose very big.

Beginners! From your first day on the rock, you have the right to inspect, and ask questions about, any system to which you're committing your life. It's a good way to learn, and a good way to stay alive. If your partner or instructor is offended, find someone else to climb with. Never change the system or the plan, however, without your partner's knowledge.

Helmets

While we can never know for certain, helmets might have made a difference in roughly 25% of the fatal and critical trauma cases. They would have significantly increased — but not guaranteed — the survival chances for five of those fatalities. Furthermore, helmets would have offered excellent protection against less serious fractures, concussions, and lacerations.

Most deaths, however, involved impacts of overwhelming force or mortal wounds other than to the head, i.e., beyond the protection offered by a helmet. This is not an argument against helmets; the point is, a helmet doesn't make you invincible. What goes on inside your head is more important than what you wear on it.

When to wear a helmet is a personal choice, but it is especially recommended for the following: beginners pushing their skills, roped solo climbing, a high risk of a bad fall or of ice fall (several El Cap routes in winter and spring), and for all approaches, descents, and climbing routes that are crowded and/or particularly loose. (See "Loose Rock," page 11.)

States of Mind

This is the key to safety. It's impossible to know how many climbers were killed by haste or overconfidence, but many survivors will tell you that they somehow lost their good judgement long enough to get hurt. It's a complex subject and sometimes a touchy one. Nevertheless, at least three states of mind frequently contribute to accidents: ignorance, casualness, and distraction.

Ignorance There is always more to learn, and even the most conscientious climber can get into trouble if unaware of the danger ("I thought it never rained . . . ") Here are some ways to fight ignorance:

• Look in the mirror. Are you the stubborn type? Do you resist suggestions? Could you be a bit overconfident? (Ask your friends.) Several partners have said of a dead friend, "I wanted to give him advice, but he always got mad when I did that. I didn't realize he was about to die."

• Read. The climbing magazines are full of good recommendations. Case histories in the American Alpine Club's *Accidents in North American Mountaineering*, a yearly compilation of accident reports, will show you how subtle factors may combine to catch you unaware. Such accounts are the next best (or worst?) thing to being there.

• Practice. Reading may make you aware but not competent. In fact, you can be dangerously misled by what you read, including this report — important details are often left out, the advice may be incorrect, and in the long run you must think and act for yourself. Several climbers, for example, waited to learn Prusiking until it was dark, raining, overhanging and they were actually in trouble. They had read about it, but they had to be rescued despite having the gear to improvise their own solutions. Book-learning alone gave them a complacency that could have proved fatal.

Casualness "I just didn't take it seriously," is a common lament. It's often correct, but it's more a symptom than a cause — there may be deeper reasons for underestimating your risk. Ignorance is one, and here are some more:

• Habit reinforcement. The more often you get away with risky business the more entrenched your lazy habits become. Have you unconsciously dropped items from your safety checklists since you were a chicken-hearted (or hare-brained) beginner?

• Your attitudes and habits can be reinforced by the experiences (and states of mind) of others. The sense of awe and commitment of the 1960's is gone from the big-wall trade routes, and young aspirants with no Grade VI's, or even V's, to their credit speak casually about them. Even for experts, most accidents on El Cap occur on the easier pitches, where their guard is down.

• Memory Decay. "I'm not going up again without raingear — I thought I would die!" A week later this climber had forgotten how scared he had been in that thunderstorm. Raingear was now too heavy and besides, he was sure he'd be able to rap off the next time. Many of us tend to forget the bad parts. We have to be hit again.

- Civilization. With fixed anchors marking the way up and ghetto blasters echoing behind, it may be hard to realize that the potential for trouble is as high in Yosemite as anywhere. Some say the possibility of fast rescue added to their casualness. Maybe, but who wants a broken leg, or worse, in the first place?

Distraction It is caused by whatever takes your mind off your work — anxiety, sore feet, skinny-dippers below — the list is endless. Being in a hurry is one of the most common causes. Here are two ways it has happened:

- Experienced climbers were often hurt after making "beginner errors" (their words) to get somewhere quickly. There was no emergency or panic, but their minds were elsewhere — on a cold beer, a good bivy, or just sick of being on that route for a week. (It's often called "summit fever.") Their mistakes were usually short cuts in protecting easy pitches, on both walls and shorter climbs. As one put it, "We were climbing as though we were on top."
- Darkness had caught two day-climbers for the first time. Unprepared, upset, and off-route, they rushed to get down, arguing with each other about what to do. After several errors, which they knew how to avoid, one died rappelling off the end of his rope.

An adequate state of mind is like good physical conditioning: it doesn't happen overnight, and it takes constant practice, but the payoff in both safety and fun is well worth it. Stay aware of your mental state: Are you uneasy before this climb? Learn to recognize that, then ask yourself why, and deal with it. Are you taking shortcuts on this pitch? Could it be you're distracted? Stop, get your act together, then go.

Rescue Despite the best of attitudes, an accident can happen to anyone. Self-rescue is often the fastest and safest way out, but whether it's the wise course of action depends on the injury and how well prepared you are. Combining with a nearby party will often give you the margin of safety you need, but do not risk aggravating an injury or getting yourself into a more serious predicament — ask for help if you need it. (Sometimes a bit of advice, delivered by loudspeaker, is all that's required.) In making your decision, keep an eye on weather and darkness — call for help early.

- If you don't have formal first aid training (which is strongly recommended), at least know how to keep an unconscious patient's airway open, how to protect a possible broken neck or back, and how to deal with external bleeding and serious blood loss. These procedures are lifesaving, do not require fancy gear, and are easy to learn.
- Head injury victims, even when unconscious, may try to untie themselves. If you have to leave one alone, make escape impossible.
- If ropes are lowered to you from a helicopter for any purpose, do not attach them to your anchors unless you are specifically instructed to do so — if the helicopter has to leave suddenly it could pull you off the wall. If you are told to anchor a rope, rescuers will be using a system that does not expose you to that risk; anchor that rope securely — it may be a rescuer's lifeline. Follow instructions exactly.

Who Pays for Rescues? The taxpayer does; the NPS does not charge for the cost of rescues, except for any ambulance services required. This is true even if you are fined by the courts for negligence, which is a separate charge altogether (see below). But rescues can be expensive and what the future holds is anybody's guess. The NPS is examining the possibility of charging all victims for the full cost of their rescues, and partial costs are charged in some parks now. This issue is complex, but it is clear that responsible behavior by those who use the park will minimize the threat.

Risk, Responsibility, and the Limits to Climbing

The NPS has no regulations specifying how you must climb. There is one regulation, however, requiring that all park users act responsibly. This applies to climbers, in that the consequences of your actions put rescuers and other climbers at risk. One rescuer has been killed in the park, so far. Thus, if your own negligence got you into trouble, you may be charged with "creating a hazardous condition" for others. As an example, a climber was fined because he became stranded by a hailstorm while attempting to free-solo the Steck-Salathé on Sentinel Rock. Storms had been predicted, and his rescue should not have been necessary.

Even avoidable accidents are understandable, thus legal charges are not frequently filed. Of all park users, however, climbers should be particularly aware — they know that their sport is dangerous, that safety lies in education and training, and that there is an information network available.

So take what you'll need with you on the climb, or have competent friends ready to back you up. The climber stranded on Sentinel, for example, could have been rescued by friends without NPS participation or knowledge — the way it must often be done on expeditions. Freedom of expression and responsibility need not be incompatible.

Climbing will always be risky. It should be clear, however, that a reduced accident rate is possible without seriously restricting the sport. The party in its fifth day on The Nose and the party passing them in its fifth hour may each be climbing safely or be blindly out of control. You have a right to choose your own climbing style and level of risk, but you owe it to yourself and everyone else to make that choice with your eyes wide open.

Other Notes

Voluntary Registration System If you wish, you may register at the Valley Visitor Center before your climb. However, the NPS does not monitor your progress at any time; the registration information you provide is used only if someone reports that you are overdue. Your best insurance is a friend who checks on you frequently.

To Report An Emergency From a public phone, dial 911. No money is needed to make the call. Stay at the phone until a ranger arrives, unless you are specifically given other instructions.

Accident/Hazard Reporting If you know of dangerous route conditions such as loose rock or bad anchors, consider posting the information on the bulletin board at Camp Four (irreverently called Sunnyside by the NPS). Your information will help other climbers.

Fixed Gear Warning The park is a Wilderness Area, not an urban climbing wall — the NPS does not inspect or maintain climbing or descent routes, including fixed anchors, loose rock or any other feature. You are strictly on your own. Recently, there have been those involved in upgrading the quality of the fixed anchors (some of which are 30 years old) that are found on many climbs. A selfless act and an incredible amount of work and expense, the result benefits all climbers. In addition, the removal of old gear has demonstrated just how unreliable fixed anchors can be. Some examples: fixed slings on Half Dome (clearly having seen repeated use as rappel anchors) were found to be simply jammed in a crack, not actually attached to anything! Relatively new ⅜-inch bolts on Middle Cathedral were found to be placed in a hole drilled too big, and held in place merely with latex caulk! Not specifically mentioned are the many old ¼-inch bolts that failed with a simple pull. If you do replace old bolts, use the same hole, and be certain of your ability to place lasting anchors.

Fixed pins should be replaced or removed before the eyes are broken.

Many single old ¼-inch bolts have been placed off-route as emergency rappel anchors over the years. They may falsely entice the novice off route and/or provide the false presumption that they provide a safe way down. These bolts should not be trusted for anything!

A great habit is to carry spare slings to replace old ones at rappel stations to help amortize route maintenance throughout the climbing community.

Tossing Haul Bags Do not throw your haul bag off a wall. You cannot always be sure the coast is clear, and the bag will drift in the wind. No one has been hurt yet, but it will happen — there have been a few close calls. Bag-tossing also creates a carnival atmosphere, a big mess (of your gear), and lots of false alarms for rescuers. (Tourists usually think it's a body.)

Sources of Information Try the local climbers, found in the parking lot at Camp Four, the bulletin board at the Camp Four kiosk, the Mountain Shop, the Visitor Center at Yosemite Village, any ranger, or the NPS library (next to the Visitor Center). The library is the home of the American Alpine Club's Sierra Nevada Branch Library. It carries magazines, journals, and books on all aspects of climbing, mountaineering, and natural history.

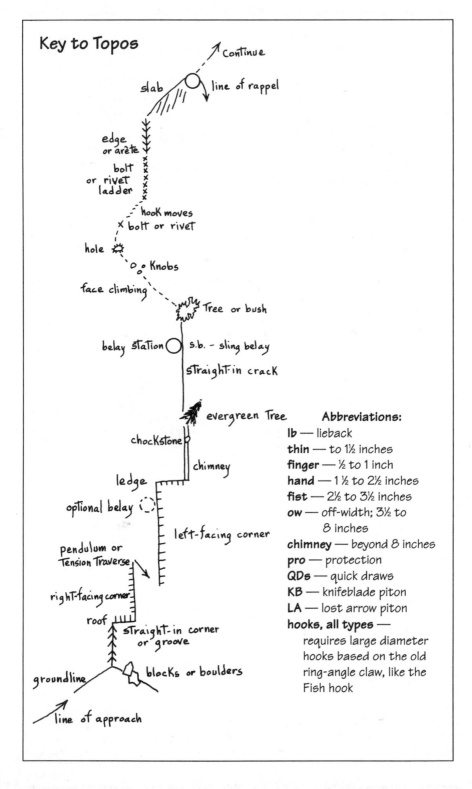

Key to Topos

Continue

slab — line of rappel

edge or arête

bolt or rivet ladder

hook moves

bolt or rivet

hole

Knobs

face climbing

Tree or bush

belay station — s.b. - sling belay

straight-in crack

evergreen Tree

chockstone

chimney

ledge

optional belay

left-facing corner

pendulum or Tension Traverse

right-facing corner

roof

straight-in corner or groove

groundline — blocks or boulders

line of approach

Abbreviations:

lb — lieback
thin — to 1½ inches
finger — ½ to 1 inch
hand — 1½ to 2½ inches
fist — 2½ to 3½ inches
ow — off-width; 3½ to 8 inches
chimney — beyond 8 inches
pro — protection
QDs — quick draws
KB — knifeblade piton
LA — lost arrow piton
hooks, all types —
   requires large diameter hooks based on the old ring-angle claw, like the Fish hook

HOW TO USE THIS BOOK

The routes in this book are arranged in geographical order, starting from the west end of the north side of the Valley. The south side follows, from east to west. The Overview Map of the valley (page 26), locates all the cliff formations. To assist in identifying the climbs on the cliffs, the photos identify the major routes. Occasionally, the photo pages may provide the sole description for obscure routes; in this case the caption will include the rating. Also, some routes that do not have topo information are included in the First Ascent appendix. On the topo page will be the route name, grade, and any unusual protection needs for the climb.The term arête is stretched far beyond its true definition. In this book it means any edge formed by two planes of rock, regardless of the mechanics of creation.

Ratings

Free Ratings The Yosemite Decimal System is used throughout this guide. Developed at Tahquitz Rock in the early 1950s and applied to great extent in Yosemite, the decimal ratings found in the Valley represent the standards by which climbs throughout the country are compared. With the continuing rise of free climbing standards, the Decimal System has ceased to be strictly decimal, and instead reflects the open-ended nature of free climbing possibilities. Today there are routes of 5.10, 5.11, 5.12 and so on, but in the early 70s, the top grade, 5.10, was considered by many to be too broad in scope, describing routes that were as varied in difficulty as 5.7 is from 5.9. Consequently, a "sub-grading" system was promoted by Jim Bridwell to further delineate between the "easiest" 5.10 and the "hardest" 5.10. This system was widely accepted and today the upper rock climbing grades will often show an a, b, c, or d suffix that further defines the difficulty. An effort was also made at that time to establish a standard for the various grades.

The Decimal System gives no information on the protection possibilities for a climb. This is left to the leader to ascertain on the lead. As a rule, on the crack climbs you are climbing your source of protection. On the face and slab routes, you must rely more on your ability to judge the terrain ahead of you.

Aid Ratings The interpretation of aid ratings is an evolving process. Differing from free ratings in that a combined measure of the technical difficulty in arranging specific placements as well as overall leader security (fall potential-consequences) are taken into account. Advances in aid climbing have necessitated certain adjustments in the closed scale used to rate aid routes. New definitions are applied to the increments of difficulty as well as a greater emphasis on a plus (+) or minus (-) suffix augmenting the standard scale.

Rock, rating, and rack are all subject to change as continuing ascents occur. The common use of hammers has obvious impact. Flakes ranging from the miniscule to monstrous sometimes break away leaving only a fresh puzzle. For better or worse the use of chisel and drill often continues beyond the first ascent of a route. Progressive scaring and an increase in fixed placements may warrant certain rack adjustments. Larger pitons become necessary, yet this situation may stabilize as placements become fixed and in extremely scarred rock TCU placement or even free climbing become possibilities. Route information becomes more accurate and ratings more objective with subsequent ascents. Beware, as many topos in this book have had few or only one ascent.

- A0 (French Free) When the climber is generally in a free climbing mode and equipment, often fixed, is grabbed or an improvised aid sling used for quick passage. Tension traverses, pendulums, and rappels often fall into this category. Placements can vary from tattered slings on an ugly bashie to a short ladder of shining bolts.

- A1 Traditionally meant "outstanding fall-catching placements," usually in well-defined cracks. This is now often stretched to include sturdy rivet ladders and good placements requiring fragile gear, such as small wired nuts, and only in controlled settings where subsequent placements become more secure.

- A2 A good familiarity with equipment options and placement is required while travelling through short sections of marginal security.

- A3 Advanced familiarity with equipment options, placement, and marginal rock (rotten, loose, and expanding), coupled with an appreciation for falls of consequence.

- A4 Modified equipment may be necessary. Exceptional skill and experience required with placement, route finding, and marginal/hazardous rock conditions while operating in situations that normally invite potential long and/or very serious falls.

- A5 Modified equipment may be necessary. An expert level of skill and experience required with placement, route finding, and marginal/hazardous rock conditions while operating in situations that normally provoke potential death falls.

Climbing the Walls

Yosemite is known for cliffs that are clean and beautifully sheer, big and plentiful. El Capitan and Half Dome are familiar to climbers the world over for their sculptured and dramatic rises of 3,000 and 2,000 feet respectively. Throughout the Valley are dozens of sheer faces that rise over 1,200 vertical feet, some in fact still unclimbed. Ascents of these big walls usually involve aid techniques, methods that are neither fast nor uncomplicated. No one appreciates the size of El Cap more than one who has spent days climbing it. The fledgling wall climber may find, however, that technical climbing prowess counts less for success than tenacity.

Pitons are still in common use for the walls, though sophisticated nuts and Friends form the backbone of the aid rack. The newer routes usually require more specialized gear and more extensive piton racks. Walls that have seen much free climbing can usually be protected without resorting to pitons. Routes like **The Nose**, **Northwest Face** of Half Dome, and **Salathé** should be respected as pitonless climbs. It is wise to carry a few copperheads and certainly a selection of hooks when venturing away from the trade routes. A bolt kit is recommended as a precaution on all walls; self-rescue is always the preferred escape, but seek retreat before blasting a way up a route that is too difficult for you. Keyhole bolt hangers, dowel and rivet hangers, and sometimes even a laddered extendible "cheater stick" are essential for using the hangerless bolts, rivets, and dowels or the newer routes. Hardware lists in this book that refer to "hooks, all types" require large diameter hooks based on the old ring-angle claw, like the currently produced Fish Hook. In an attempt to keep the rock resource alive a little longer, a minimal use of copperhead chiseling is urged.

From the standpoint of fighting litter, it is imperative to carry down what is carried up. Old slings, wads of tape, and assorted wall trash found at the base of obscure and remote cliffs discredit the notion that climbers are actively respectful of the natural environment. Few issues threatened the climber's freedom as seriously as littering. Officially, Park Service policy says that anything above 4,200 feet is wilderness and everything that is carried in should be packed out.

Due to the need to protect the nesting habitat of the peregrine falcon, the routes on El Cap from **Pacific Ocean** inclusive to **Tangerine Trip** are off-limits to climbing from January 1 to August 1.

Yosemite Valley Overview Map

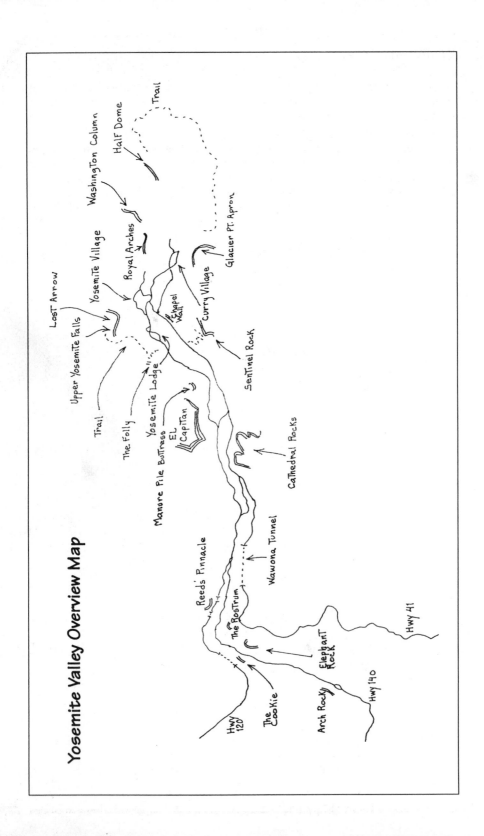

Ribbon Falls Amphitheater

1. Gold Wall
2. Hole in the Sky
3. Dyslexia

4. Keel Haul
5. Solar Power Arête
6. Gold Ribbon

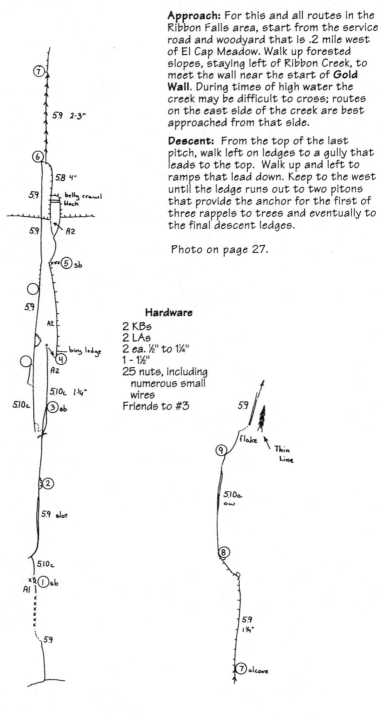

Approach: For this and all routes in the Ribbon Falls area, start from the service road and woodyard that is .2 mile west of El Cap Meadow. Walk up forested slopes, staying left of Ribbon Creek, to meet the wall near the start of **Gold Wall**. During times of high water the creek may be difficult to cross; routes on the east side of the creek are best approached from that side.

Descent: From the top of the last pitch, walk left on ledges to a gully that leads to the top. Walk up and left to ramps that lead down. Keep to the west until the ledge runs out to two pitons that provide the anchor for the first of three rappels to trees and eventually to the final descent ledges.

Photo on page 27.

Hardware

2 KBs
2 LAs
2 ea. ½" to 1¼"
1 - 1½"
25 nuts, including numerous small wires
Friends to #3

VI 5.10b A3

Approach: See page 28.

Photo on page 27.

Hardware
2 beaks
2 rurps
15 KBs
15 LAs
3 ea. ½" and ⅝"
1 - ¾"
20 heads, mostly #2
  and #3
hooks, pointed
  Chouinards and Fish
3 ea. TCUs
Friends:
  3 ea. to #3
  2 ea. #3.5 and #4
  1 - #4 Camalot

⑨
A2
"The Fist"
⑧
5.9
A1 ⑦
A3
×⑥
A3
⑤
A1
A3
④
A2
③
A2
②
5.10b
①
3rd
Ribbon Falls
Amphitheater
Talus mound
Ribbon
Falls

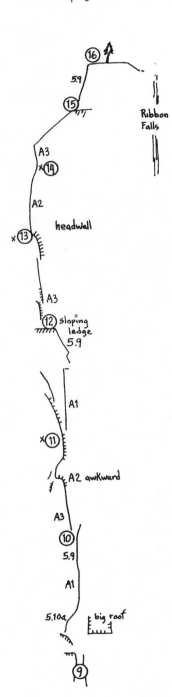

⑯
5.9
⑮
Ribbon
Falls
A3
×⑭
A2
headwall
×⑬
A3
⑫ sloping
  ledge
5.9
A1
×⑪
A2 awkward
A3
⑩
5.9
A1
5.10a big roof
⑨

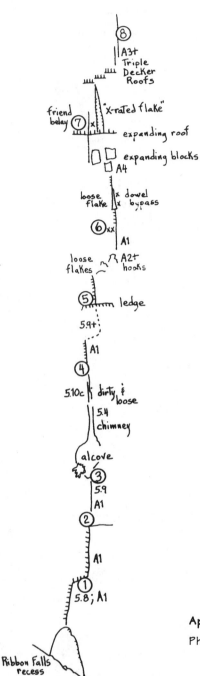

⑧ A3+
Triple
Decker
Roofs

"X-rated flake"

friend
belay ⑦ x
expanding roof

expanding blocks

☐ ☐
☐ A4

loose   x dowel
flake   x bypass

⑥ xx
A1

loose   A2+
flakes   hooks

⑤ ledge

5.9+

A1

④
5.10c dirty &
       loose

5.4
chimney

alcove

③
5.9
A1

②

A1

①
5.8; A1

Ribbon Falls
recess

Approach: See page 28.

Photo on page 27.

5.6

⑮ dead Tree

5.8

⑭

5.8

⑬

5.8

⑫

Keel Haul

4th & 5th
class

⑪

4th class

⑩ 5.4

5.7 chimney

A1

5.10d

⑨

A1 (short)

⑧

Hardware
2 rurps
15 KBs
20 LAs
8 ea. ½" to ¾"
4 - 1"
2 ea. 1¼" to 1½"
wires
cams:
  2 ea. #0.4 to #3
  1 - #3.5
  2 - #4
  2 heads
hooks, all types

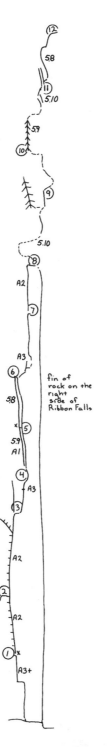

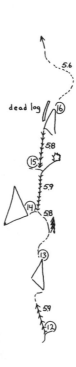

Approach: See page 28.

Descent: Hike east along the rim of the valley, and pick up the trail that leads north off the top of El Capitan toward Tamarack Flat Campground.

Hardware
1 - 3"
3 ea. 2½"
2 - 2"
standard wall rack

Photo on page 27.

fin of rock on the right side of Ribbon Falls

dead log

Approach: See page 28.

Photo on page 27.

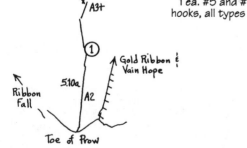

⑲ ──── ☁☁
easy
5Th

⑱ ↑ dead
Tree

5.7

⑰

5.7

⑯

5.7

5.7

⑮

5.7

⑬ 5Th   ⑭ ☁☁

x⑥

A1

⑤

expanding A2 & loose

A1

x④

follows
Corner
on
prow

"The
Bug
Eater"
A2

③

A2

x②

↓

x A3+

①

Gold Ribbon &
Vain Hope

Ribbon
Fall

5.10a

A2

Toe of Prow

Hardware

8 KBs
7 bugaboos
10 LAs
3 ea. ½" and ⅝"
2 ea. ¾" to 1"
wires, including 2 ea. RPs
cams:
    3 ea. #0.4 to #3
    2 ea. #3.5 and #4
    1 ea. #5 and #6
hooks, all types

⑬ notch

ridge →   ⑫

5.8+

A2 expanding
5.8

x⑪

A3 hooks &
free

5.7 groove

⑩

A2+ expanding

A2+

x⑨

A1

⑧

A3

⑦ x

5.8   6"
A2

"Fear of
God"

x⑥

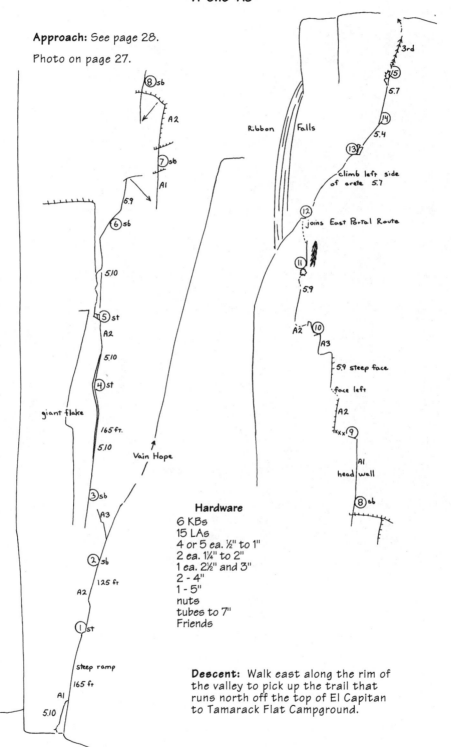

Approach: See page 28.

Photo on page 27.

⑧ sb

A2

⑦ sb

A1

5.9

⑥ sb

5.10

⑤ st

A2

5.10

④ st

giant flake

165 ft.

5.10

③ sb

A3

② sb

125 ft

A2

① st

steep ramp

165 ft

A1

5.10

Vain Hope

Ribbon Falls

→ 3rd

⑮

5.7

⑭

5.4

⑬

climb left side
of arete 5.7

⑫

joins East Portal Route

⑪

5.9

A2 ⑩

A3

5.9 steep face

face left

A2

xxx ⑨

A1
head wall

⑧ sb

Hardware
6 KBs
15 LAs
4 or 5 ea. ½" to 1"
2 ea. 1¼" to 2"
1 ea. 2½" and 3"
2 - 4"
1 - 5"
nuts
tubes to 7"
Friends

Descent: Walk east along the rim of
the valley to pick up the trail that
runs north off the top of El Capitan
to Tamarack Flat Campground.

El Capitan – West Face

1. West Face (5.11c)
2. Mr. Midwest
3. Realm of the Flying Monkeys
4. Mirage
5. Lurking Fear

Approach Park 0.1 mile west of the El Capitan Bridge. Take the climber's trail that heads back through the woods directly toward The Nose. Beneath that route, the trail divides, leading along both sides of the cliff. For routes in the **Zodiac** area, a more direct but strenuous approach ascends talus directly above a fenced area 2.1 miles west of the gas station.

For the climbs beyond the **Aquarian Wall**, skirt the scruffy gray barrier by dropping down and around the corner to a 3rd class path that leads up. To proceed further up the West Chimney, for **Mirage** and the **West Face**, stay left of the main chimney on a 3rd class rib until above the chockstone.

West of El Capitan are two prominent gullies separated by a long, brushy serrated ridge. The left gully is El Capitan Gully. It is in large part a talus slope, although exposed 3rd class slabs must be negotiated before the rim can be reached. Among the many pinnacles of the ridge to the east, one spire stands out most prominently. The is K-P Pinnacle. Its summit is easily reached with east 5th class climbing from the east. The gully/chimney that lies immediately below the West Face of El Cap is the West Chimney. Most of the large chockstones that occasionally block the gully can be avoided with circuitous and exposed scrambling. At its top, the West Chimney ends atop the K-P Pinnacle ridge where a short rappel leads west into the El Capitan Gully.

Descent Most climbers descend from the top of El Cap to the Valley floor by one of the following ways: 1: Hike up several hundred yards to the rounded summit knoll and pick up the trail that heads back into the woods. The campground off the Tuolumne road at Tamarack Flat can be reached after about 8 miles of rolling but mostly gentle downhill hiking. Consult a map. 2. From the woods behind El Cap a trail can be taken east along the rim past Eagle Peak to the Yosemite Falls Trail for a descent directly to Camp Four. The Falls Trail part of this eight mile alternative is grueling in it continuous steepness. 3. The East Ledges descent requires some 3rd class scrambling and some rappels but does offer the advantages of being snow-free in the early season and being only about 2½ hours to the Valley floor. See page 109.

Mr. Midwest
VI 5.10 A3+

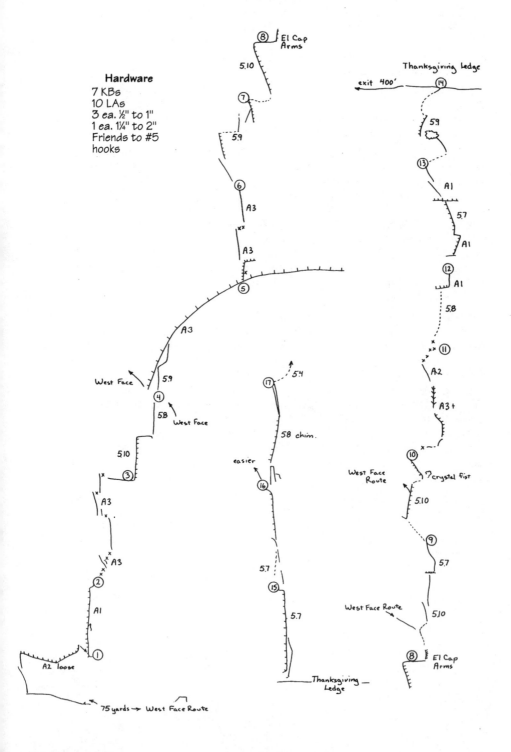

Hardware
7 KBs
10 LAs
3 ea. ½" to 1"
1 ea. 1¼" to 2"
Friends to #5
hooks

El Cap Arms

5.10

5.9

A3

A3

A3

West Face   5.9

West Face

5.8

5.10

A3

A3

A1

A2 loose

75 yards → West Face Route

5.4

5.8 chim.

easier

5.7

5.7

Thanksgiving Ledge

Thanksgiving Ledge

exit 400'

5.9

A1

5.7

A1

A1

5.8

A2

A3+

crystal fist

West Face Route

5.10

5.7

West Face Route

5.10

El Cap Arms

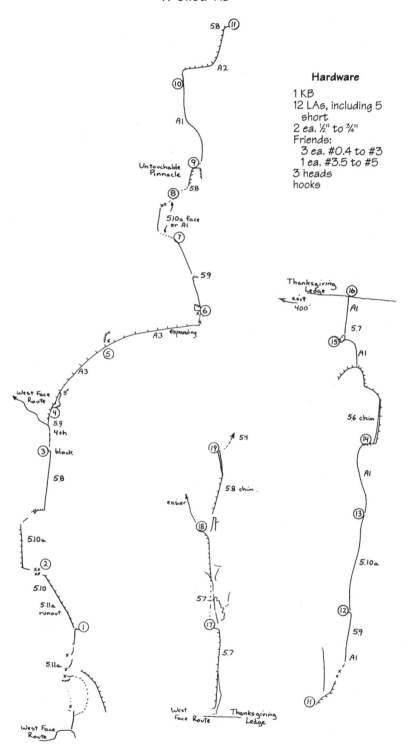

Hardware

1 KB
12 LAs, including 5
 short
2 ea. ½" to ¾"
Friends:
 3 ea. #0.4 to #3
 1 ea. #3.5 to #5
3 heads
hooks

5.8 ⑪
A2
⑩
A1
Untouchable ⑨
Pinnacle
5.8
⑧ xx
510a face
or A1
⑦
5.9
⑥ xx
A3 Expanding
✗x ⑤
A3
West Face 5'
Route ④
5.9
4th
③ block
5.8
5.10a
xx ②
xx
5.10
5.11a
runout
①
✗
5.11a ✗
✗
West Face
Route

54
⑲
5.8 chim.
easier
⑱
5.7
5.7 ⑰
5.7
West
Face Route   Thanksgiving
Ledge

Thanksgiving
Ledge ⑯
exit
400' A1
5.7
⑮ A1
5.6 chim
⑭
A1
⑬
5.10a
⑫
5.9
A1
✗
⑪ ✗

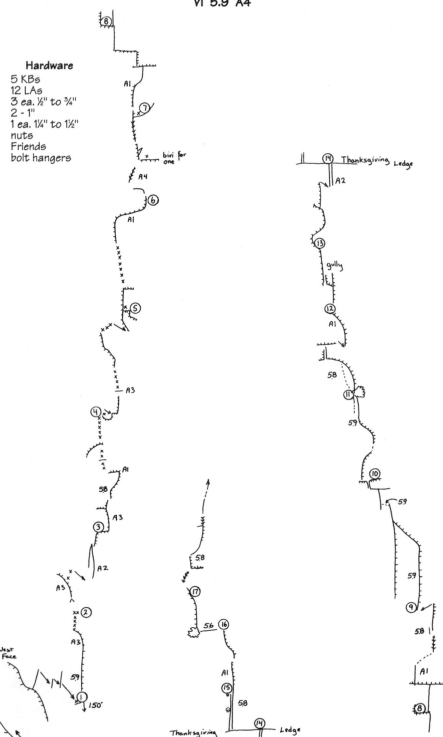

Hardware

5 KBs
12 LAs
3 ea. ½" to ¾"
2 - 1"
1 ea. 1¼" to 1½"
nuts
Friends
bolt hangers

Lurking Fear
VI 5.10 A3

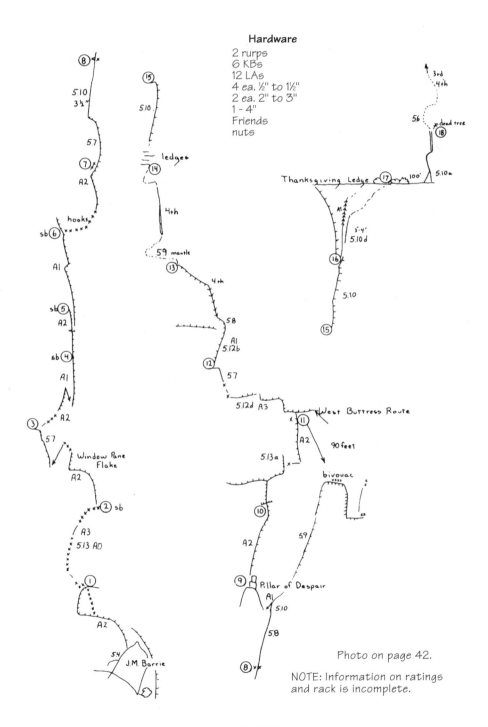

Hardware

2 rurps
6 KBs
12 LAs
4 ea. ½" to 1½"
2 ea. 2" to 3"
1 - 4"
Friends
nuts

8
5.10
3½"
5.7
7
A2
hooks
sb 6
A1
sb 5
A2
sb 4
A1
3
5.7
A2
Window Pane
Flake
A2
2 sb
A3
5.13 A0
1
A2
5.4
J.M. Barrie

15
5.10
14 ledges
4th
5.9 mantle
13
4th
5.8
A1
5.12b
12
5.7
5.12d A3
11
A2
5.13a
bivouac
10
A2
5.9
9 Pillar of Despair
A1
5.10
5.8
8

3rd
4th
5.6
dead tree
18
Thanksgiving Ledge 17 100' 5.10a
A1
3'-4"
5.10d
16
5.10
15
West Buttress Route
90 feet

Photo on page 42.

NOTE: Information on ratings
and rack is incomplete.

Photo on page 44.

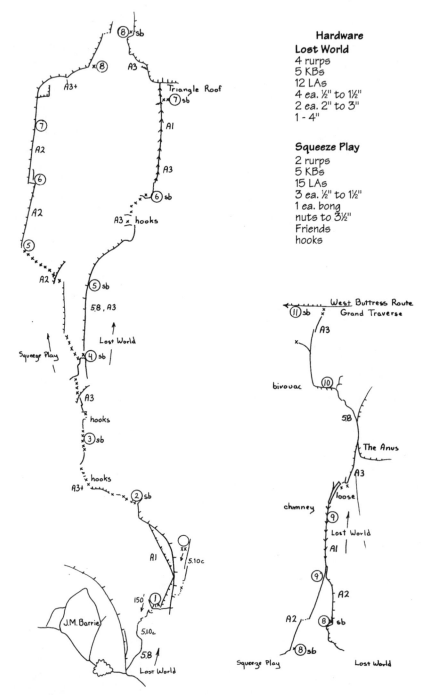

Hardware

Lost World
4 rurps
5 KBs
12 LAs
4 ea. ½" to 1½"
2 ea. 2" to 3"
1 - 4"

Squeeze Play
2 rurps
5 KBs
15 LAs
3 ea. ½" to 1½"
1 ea. bong
nuts to 3½"
Friends
hooks

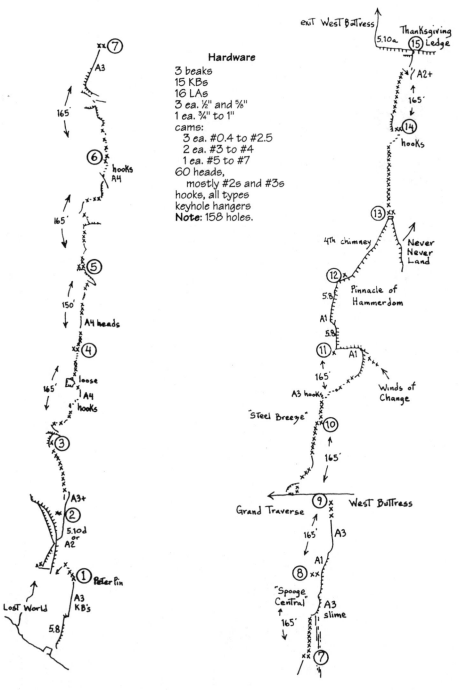

Hardware

3 beaks
15 KBs
16 LAs
3 ea. ½" and ⅝"
1 ea. ¾" to 1"
cams:
   3 ea. #0.4 to #2.5
   2 ea. #3 to #4
   1 ea. #5 to #7
60 heads,
   mostly #2s and #3s
hooks, all types
keyhole hangers
Note: 158 holes.

Photo on page 44.

El Capitan:
Southwest Face

1. Lurking Fear
2. West Buttress
3. Wings of Steel
4. Horse Chute/
   Horse Play
5. Cosmos
6. The Heart Route
7. Salathé Wall
8. The Shield

El Capitan:
Southwest Face

9. Lost World/
   Squeeze Play
10. Hole World
11. For Your Eyes Only
    (aka Octopussy)
12. Never Never Land
13. Aquarian Wall
14. Dihedral Wall
15. Excalibur
16. Bermuda Dunes
17. Son of Heart
    (aka Heart Woute)
18. Muir Wall
19. Magic Mushroom
20. The Nose

Photo on page 42.

NOTE: Information on ratings and rack is incomplete.

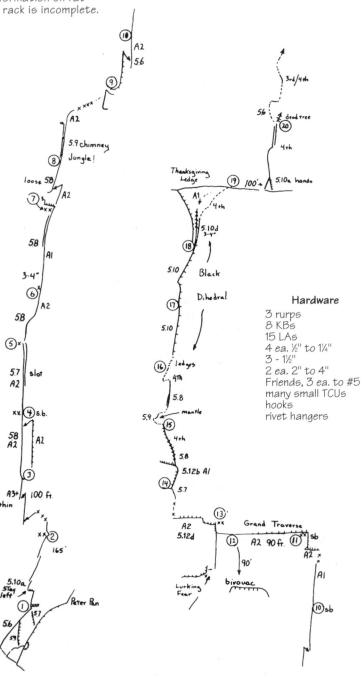

⑩ A2
5.6

⑨

××× A2

5.9 chimney
⑧ Jungle!

loose 5.8
⑦ A2
×××

5.8
A1

3-4"
⑥ A2
5.8

⑤×

5.7 slot
A2

×× ④ s.b.

5.8   A2
A2

③

A3+ 100 ft.
thin
××
×× ②
165'

5.10a
Stay
left
① ××× 5.7   Peter Pan
5.6
5.9

3rd/4th

5.6 dead tree
⑳

4th

Thanksgiving
Ledge   ⑲ 100' 5.10a hands

A1
4th
5.10d
⑱ 3-4"

5.10   Black

Dihedral
⑰

5.10

⑯ ledges
4th
5.8

5.9   mantle
⑮
4th
5.8
5.12b A1
⑭ 5.7
×

⑬
×× Grand Traverse
A2
5.12d   ⑫ A2 90ft. ⑪ sb
A2 ×
90'
bivouac   A1
Lurking
Fear
⑩ sb

Hardware
3 rurps
8 KBs
15 LAs
4 ea. ½" to 1¼"
3 - 1½"
2 ea. 2" to 4"
Friends, 3 ea. to #5
many small TCUs
hooks
rivet hangers

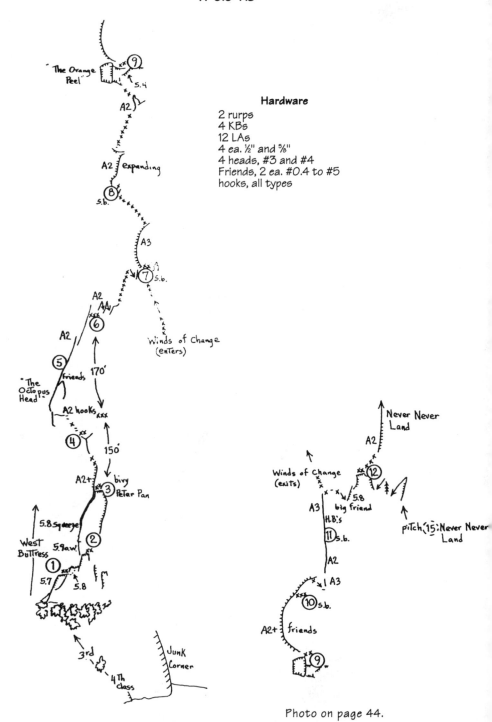

Hardware

2 rurps
4 KBs
12 LAs
4 ea. ½" and ⅝"
4 heads, #3 and #4
Friends, 2 ea. #0.4 to #5
hooks, all types

"The Orange Peel"

⑨ 5.4

A2

A2 expanding

⑧ s.b.

A3

⑦ s.b.

A2
AA
⑥

A2

Winds of Change (enters)

⑤ friends 170'

"The Octopus Head!"

A2 hooks

④ 150'

A2+ bivy Peter Pan ③

5.8 squeeze

West Buttress

5.9 a.w. ②

① 5.7 5.8

3rd

4th class

Junk Corner

Never Never Land

A2

Winds of Change (exits) ⑫ 5.8

A3 big friend

H.B.'s

⑪ s.b.

pitch 15: Never Never Land

A2

A3

⑩ s.b.

A2+ friends

⑨

Photo on page 44.

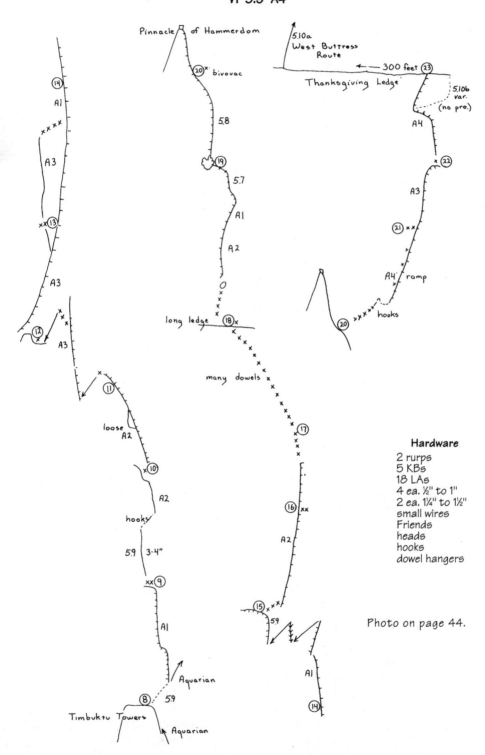

Pinnacle of Hammerdom

⑳ bivouac

5.8

⑲

5.7

A1

A2

long ledge ⑱

many dowels

⑭

A1

A3

×× ⑬

A3

⑫

A3

⑪

loose
A2

×⑩

A2

hooks

5.9 | 3-4"

×× ⑨

A1

Aquarian

⑧ 5.9

Timbuktu Towers

Aquarian

5.10a
West Buttress
Route

← 300 feet ⑳

Thanksgiving Ledge

5.10b
var.
(no pro.)

A4

× ㉒

A3

㉑ ××

A4 ramp

⑳ ×××× hooks

⑰

⑯ ××

A2

⑮ ××

5.9

A1

⑭

Hardware

2 rurps
5 KBs
18 LAs
4 ea. ½" to 1"
2 ea. 1¼" to 1½"
small wires
Friends
heads
hooks
dowel hangers

Photo on page 44.

Hardware

1 rurp
4 KBs
10 LAs
4 ea. ½" to 1½"
3 - 2"
Friends to #4
nuts
rivet hangers

Photo on page 44.

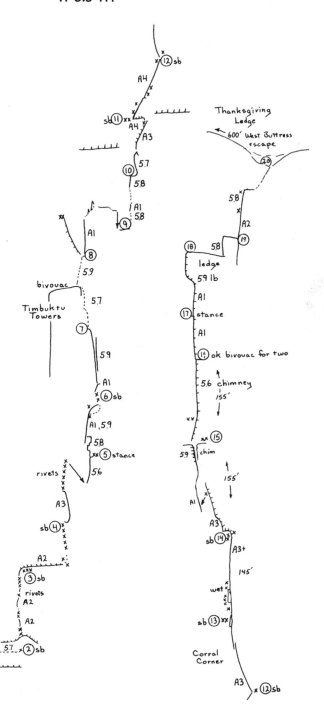

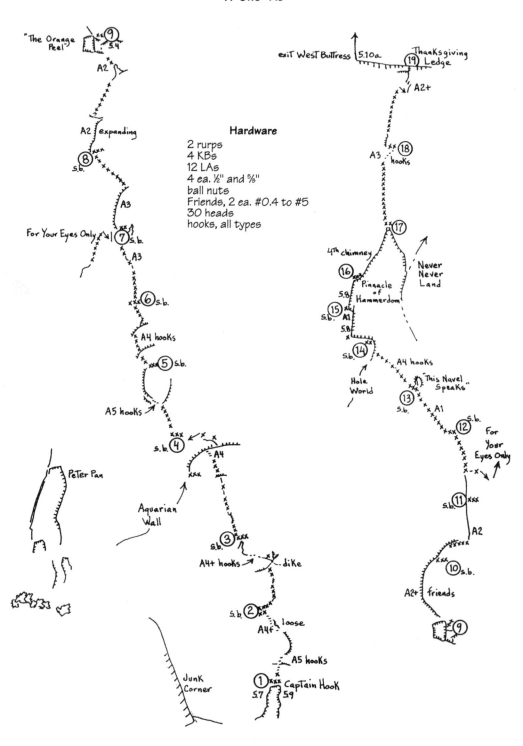

Hardware

2 rurps
4 KBs
12 LAs
4 ea. ½" and ⅝"
ball nuts
Friends, 2 ea. #0.4 to #5
30 heads
hooks, all types

Photo on page 42.

Hardware

5 rurps
5 KBs
5 LAs
3 ea. ½" to ¾"
4 - 1"
8 - 1¼"
3 - 1½"
1 ea. 2" to 4"
small wires
Friends, including 2 ea. #3
 and #4
40 heads
hooks, all types
rivet loops
Aquarian Wall rack

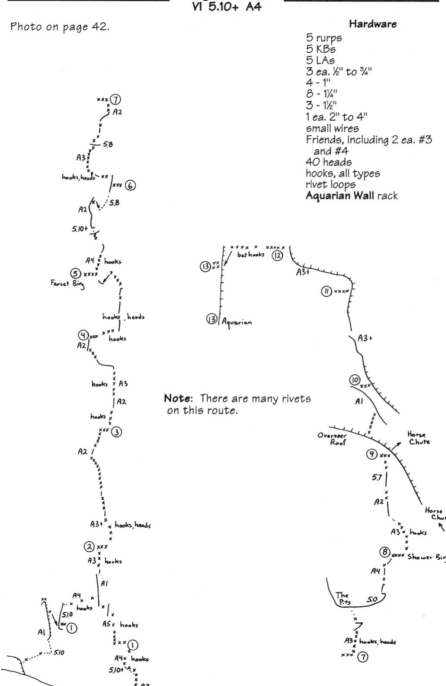

Note: There are many rivets on this route.

Horse Chute
VI 5.9 A3
Horse Play
VI 5.9 A3

Photo on page 42.

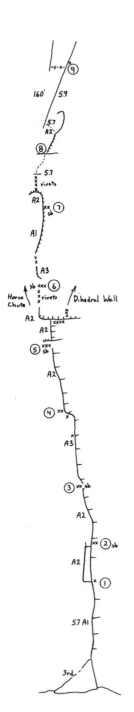

Hardware

Horse Chute:
3 rurps
2 KBs
25 LAs
4 - ½"
6 ea. ⅝" to 1¼"
1 ea. 1½" to 2½"
Friends, 2 ea.
wires
rivet hangers

Horse Play:
Same rack as **Horse Chute** plus 10 heads,
  mostly small.

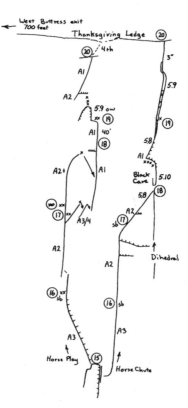

Photo on page 44.

NOTE: Information on ratings and rack is incomplete.

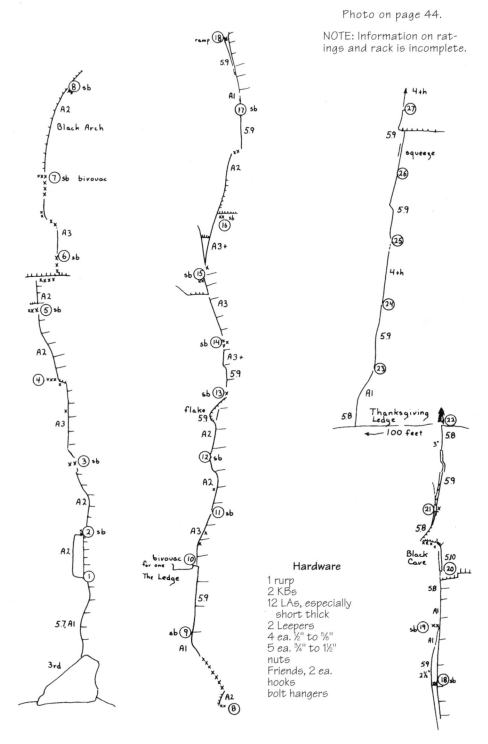

Hardware

1 rurp
2 KBs
12 LAs, especially
  short thick
2 Leepers
4 ea. ½" to ⅝"
5 ea. ¾" to 1½"
nuts
Friends, 2 ea.
hooks
bolt hangers

Photo on page 42.

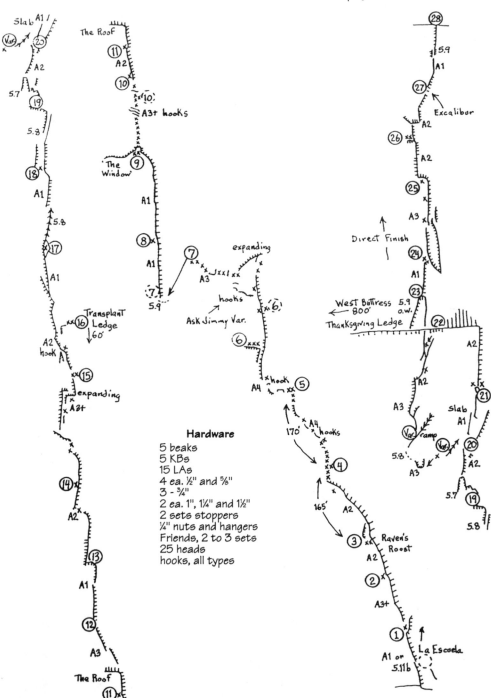

Slab A1
Var.
20
A2
5.7
19
5.8
18
A1
5.8
17
A1
Transplant
Ledge
16   ↓60'
A2
hook
15
expanding
A3+
14
A2
13
A1
12
A3
The Roof
11

The Roof
11
A2
10
'10'
A3+ hooks
The
Window
9
A1
8
A1
7
A3 Jxx1xx   expanding
'7'
5.9   hooks
Ask Jimmy Var.
6
6
A4 hook 5
170' A4 hooks
4
165' A2
3 Raven's
A2   Roost
2
A3+
1
A1 or La Escuela
5.11b

Hardware
5 beaks
5 KBs
15 LAs
4 ea. ½" and ⅝"
3 - ¾"
2 ea. 1", 1¼" and 1½"
2 sets stoppers
¼" nuts and hangers
Friends, 2 to 3 sets
25 heads
hooks, all types

28
5.9
A1
27
Excalibur
A2
26
A2
25
A3
Direct Finish
24
A1
23
West Buttress 5.9
← 800'   o.w.
Thanksgiving Ledge
22
A2
A2
A3
Slab
Var. ramp   A1
5.8   Var.
A3   20
A2
5.7   19
5.8
21

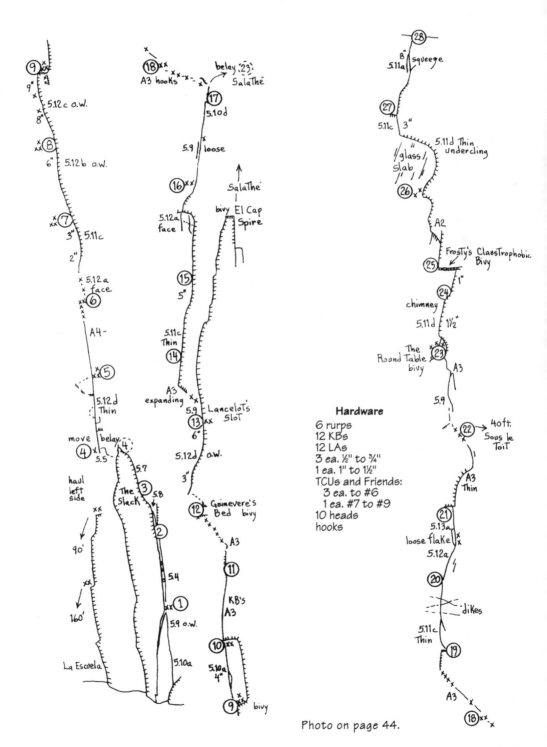

The topo diagram shows the route with the following labeled features:

- 28, 8" squeeze, 5.11a
- 27, 5.11c, 3"
- 5.11d Thin undercling
- glass slab
- 26, A2
- Frosty's Claustrophobic Bivy
- 25
- 24, 1", chimney, 5.11d, 1½"
- The Round Table bivy
- 23, A3
- 5.9
- 22, 40ft. Sous le Toit
- A3 Thin
- 21, 5.13a, loose flake, 5.12a
- 20, dikes
- 5.11c Thin
- 19, A3
- 18, xx

- 18, A3 hooks, xx
- belay (23) Salathé
- 17, 5.10d
- 5.9 loose
- 16, xx, Salathé
- bivy, El Cap Spire
- 5.12a face, 15, 5"
- 5.11c Thin, 14
- A3 expanding, 5.9, Lancelot's Slot
- 13, xx, 6"
- 5.12d o.w., 3"
- 12, Guinevere's Bed bivy
- A3
- 11, KB's, A3
- 5.4
- 1, 5.9 o.w.
- 10, xx, 5.10a, 4"
- 9, bivy
- 5.10a

- 9, xx, 9"
- 5.12c o.w., 8"
- 8, xx, 6", 5.12b o.w.
- 7, xx, 3", 5.11c, 2"
- 5.12a face, 6, xx
- A4-
- 5, xx
- 5.12d Thin
- move belay, 4, 5.5
- haul left side
- The Slack, 3, 5.7, 5.8
- 2
- 90'
- 160'
- La Escuela

Hardware
6 rurps
12 KBs
12 LAs
3 ea. ½" to ¾"
1 ea. 1" to 1½"
TCUs and Friends:
  3 ea. to #6
  1 ea. #7 to #9
10 heads
hooks

Photo on page 44.

Photo on page 44.

Hardware

10 rurps
20 KBs
20 LAs
4 ea. ½" to 1"
1 ea. 1¼" to 1½"
1 ea. 5" to 7" tubes
wires
Friends, 4 ea.
  including one #5
hooks

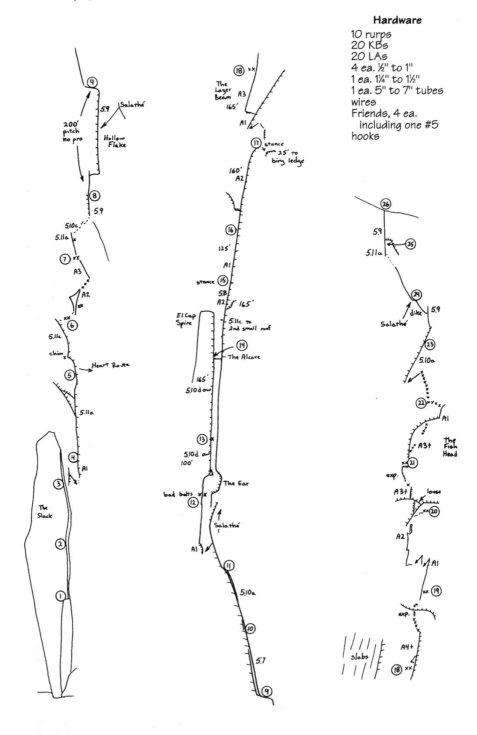

Photo on page 42.

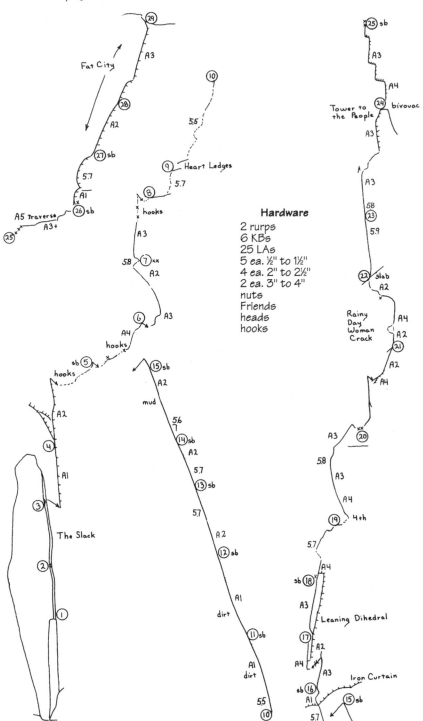

Fat City

29

A3

28

A2

27 sb

5.7

A1

A5 traverse

26 sb

A3+

25

10

5.5

9 Heart Ledges

5.7

8

hooks

A3

5.8 7 xx

A2

6 A3

A4

hooks

sb 5

hooks

A2

4

A1

3

The Slack

2

1

15 sb

A2

mud

5.6

14 sb

A2

5.7

13 sb

5.7

A2

12 sb

A1

dirt

11 sb

A1

dirt

5.5

10

Hardware

2 rurps
6 KBs
25 LAs
5 ea. ½" to 1½"
4 ea. 2" to 2½"
2 ea. 3" to 4"
nuts
Friends
heads
hooks

25 sb

A3

A4

Tower to
the People

24 bivouac

A3

A3

5.8

23

5.9

22 slab

A2

Rainy
Day
Woman
Crack

A4

A2

21

A2

A4

xx

A3 20

5.8

A3

A4

19 4th

5.7

sb 18

A4

A3

Leaning Dihedral

17

A2

A4

A3

Iron Curtain

sb 16

A1

15 sb

5.7

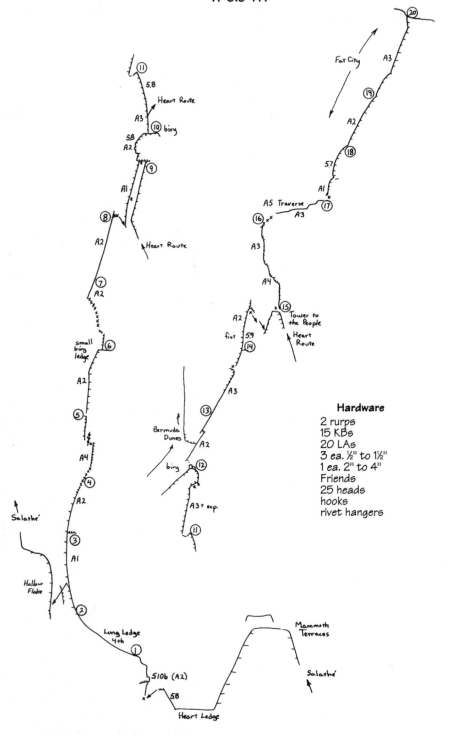

Hardware

2 rurps
15 KBs
20 LAs
3 ea. ½" to 1½"
1 ea. 2" to 4"
Friends
25 heads
hooks
rivet hangers

Photo on page 44.

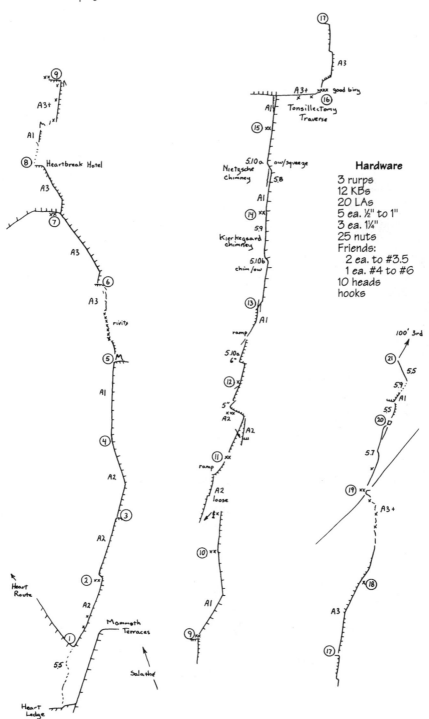

Hardware

3 rurps
12 KBs
20 LAs
5 ea. ½" to 1"
3 ea. 1¼"
25 nuts
Friends:
  2 ea. to #3.5
  1 ea. #4 to #6
10 heads
hooks

Hardware

5 rurps
15 KBs
15 LAs
3 ea. ½" to ¾"
2 ea. 1" to 1½"
wired nuts
30 heads
hooks, all types
RP and rivet hangers
Friends:
  2 ea. to #3
  1 ea. #3.5 to #4

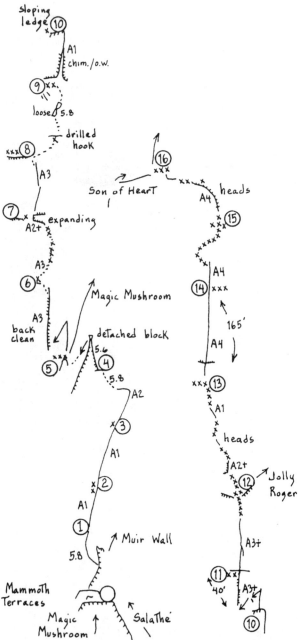

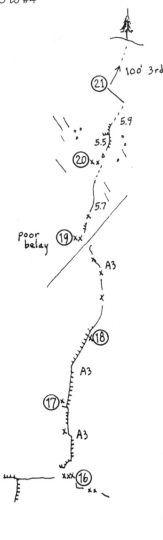

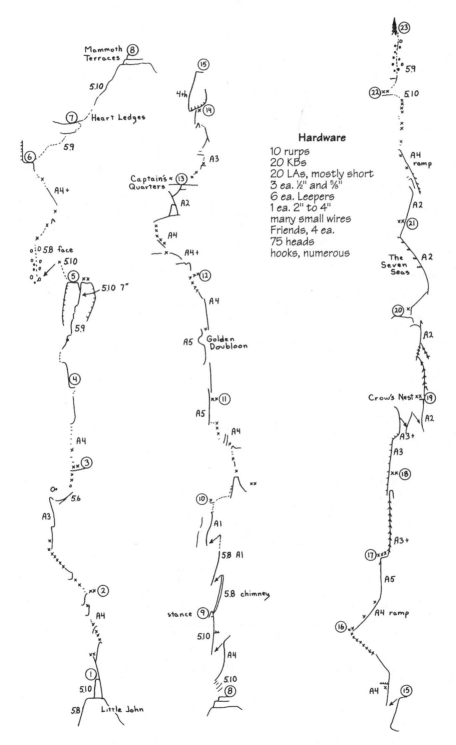

Mammoth Terraces ⑧

5.10

⑦ Heart Ledges

5.9

⑥

A4+

0 5.8 face
0 0
× 5.10
0 0
0 0

⑤ ××

5.10 7"

5.9

④

A4

×× ③

0 5.6

A3

×× ②

A4

①

5.10

5.8   Little John

⑮

4th

× ⑭

A3

Captain's ×⑬
Quarters

A2

A4

A4+

×× ⑫

A4

A5 ⟨ Golden
       Doubloon

×× ⑪

A5

A4

⑩

A1

5.8 A1

5.8 chimney

stance ⑨

5.10

A4

5.10

⑧

Hardware

10 rurps
20 KBs
20 LAs, mostly short
3 ea. ½" and ⅝"
6 ea. Leepers
1 ea. 2" to 4"
many small wires
Friends, 4 ea.
75 heads
hooks, numerous

⑳ ×

⑨ ×× ⑳ 5.9

㉒ ×× 5.10

A4
ramp

A2

×× ㉑

The
Seven   A2
Seas

⑳ ×

A2

Crow's Nest ×× ⑲

A2

A3+

A3

×× ⑱

A3+

⑰ ×××

A5

A4 ramp

⑯ ×

A4 ×   ⑮

Photo on page 44.

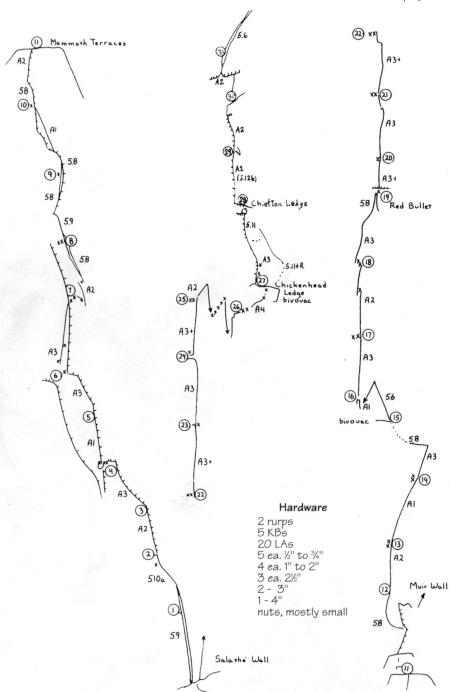

11 Mammoth Terraces
A2
5.8
10 x
A1
5.8
9 x
5.8
5.9
xx 8
5.8
7 x
A2
A3 x
6 x
A3
5
A1
4
A3
3
A2
2
5.10a
1
5.9

5.6
3
A2
3.5
A2
29
A2
(5.12b)
28 ChiefTon Ledge
5.11
A3
27
25 xx   A2
26 x A4
A3+
24
A3
23 x
A3+
xx 22

Chickenhead
Ledge
bivouac
5.11+R

22 xx
A3+
xx 21
A3
20 x
A3+
19
5.8   Red Bullet
A3
18
A2
xx 17
A3
16   5.6
A1
bivouac   15
5.8
A3
x 14
A1
x 13
A2
12
Muir Wall
5.8
11

Salathé Wall

Hardware
2 rurps
5 KBs
20 LAs
5 ea. ½" to ¾"
4 ea. 1" to 2"
3 ea. 2½"
2 - 3"
1 - 4"
nuts, mostly small

Photo on page 42.

Hardware

6 rurps
5 KBs
15 LAs
5 ea. ½"
7 ea. ⅝"
4 ea. ¾", sawed-off
3 ea. 1"
2 ea. 1¼"
1 - 1½"
wires, 2 to 3 sets
Friends, 2 ea.
20 copperheads
hooks, all types
sawed-off angles useful

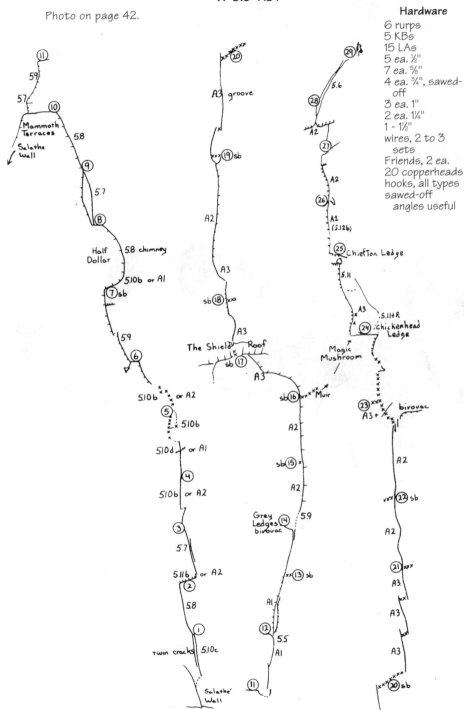

Dorn Direct
(to Shield)
VI 5.9 A4

Hardware

10 rurps
20 KBs
20 LAs
4 ea. ½" to 1"
2 ea. 1¼" to 1½"
nuts
Friends
hooks
bolt hangers
rivet hangers

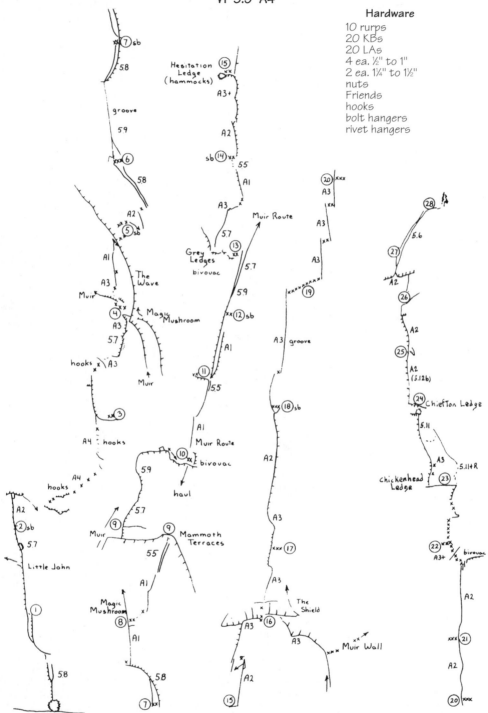

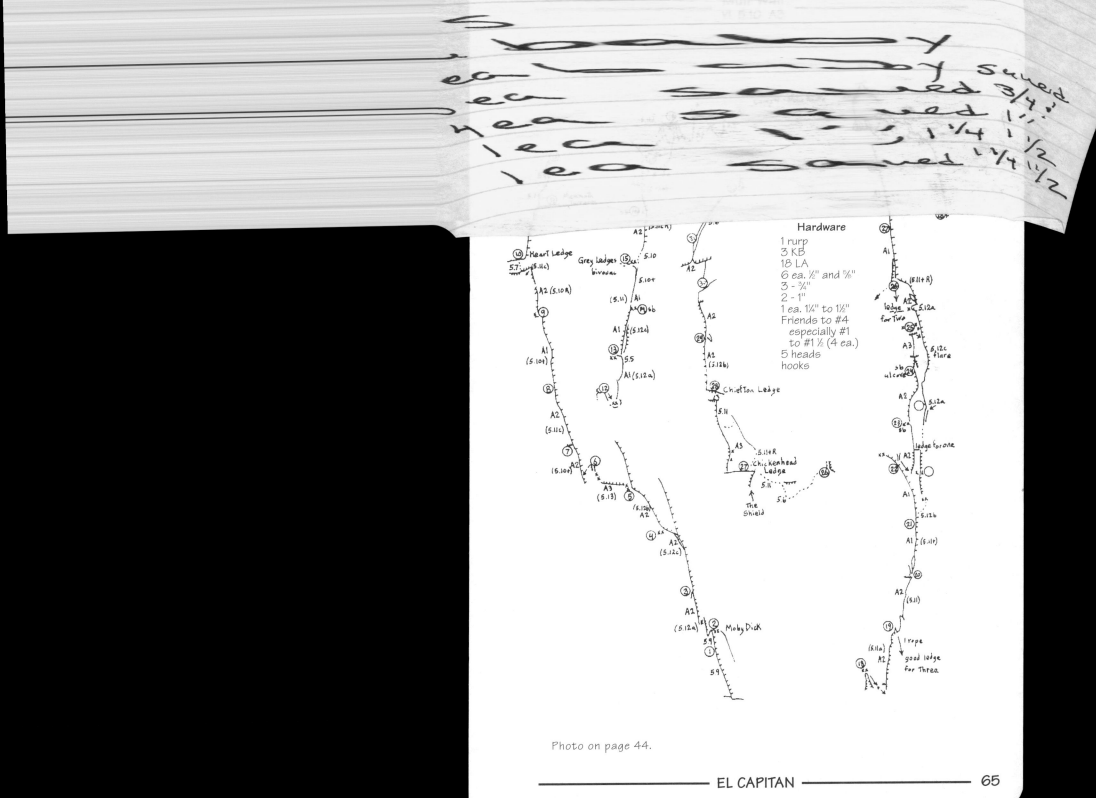

Hardware

1 rurp
3 KB
18 LA
6 ea. ½" and ⅝"
3 - ¾"
2 - 1"
1 ea. 1¼" to 1½"
Friends to #4
  especially #1
  to #1 ½ (4 ea.)
5 heads
hooks

Photo on page 44.

Photo on page 42.

Hardware

Bring many pieces from very small to 3½" (optional 6" to 8" for Hollow Flake). This route is often fixed from Heart Ledge. Bolt stations and 4½ ropes meet the ground via the left side of Little John.

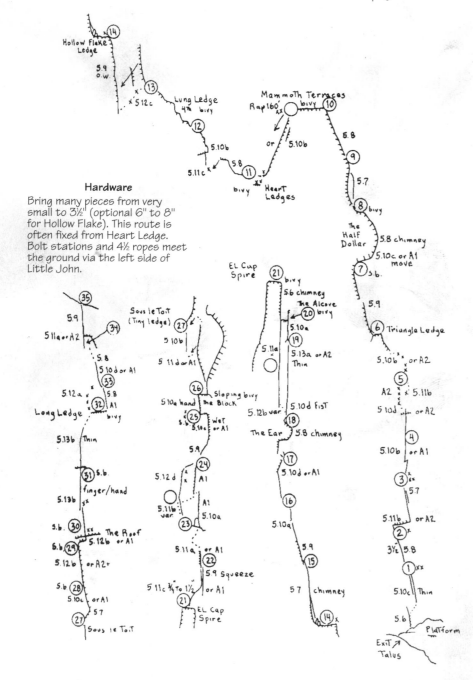

Hollow Flake Ledge

5.9 o.w.

(14)

(13) x 5.12c

Lung Ledge 4th bivy

(12)

5.10b

5.11c 5.8 (11) bivy

Mammoth Terraces bivy (10)
Rap 160'

or 5.10b

5.8

(9)

5.7

(8) bivy

The Half Dollar

5.8 chimney

5.10c or A1 move

(7) s.b.

5.9

Heart Ledges

El Cap Spire

(21) bivy

5.6 chimney

The Alcove (20) bivy

5.10a

(19)

5.11a

5.13a or A2 Thin

(6) Triangle Ledge

5.10b or A2

(5)

A2 5.11b

5.10d or A2

(4)

5.10b or A1

(3)

5.7

5.11b or A2

(2)

3½ 5.8

(1) xx

5.10c Thin

5.6

Platform

Exit Talus

(35)

5.9

(34)

5.11a or A2

Sous le Toit (Tiny ledge) (27)

5.10b

5.11d or A1

5.8

5.10d or A1

(33)

5.12a 5.8

(32) A1

Long Ledge bivy

5.13b Thin

(31) s.b.

finger/hand

5.13b

s.b. (30) xx The Roof

s.b. (29) 5.12b or A1

5.12b or A2+

s.b. (28)

5.10c or A1

(27) 5.7

Sous le Toit

(26) Sloping bivy The Block

5.10a hand

(25) Wet or A1

5.9

(24) A1

5.12d A1

5.11b var

(23) A1 5.10a

5.11a or A1

(22)

5.9 Squeeze or A1

5.11c ¾ To 1½ (21) El Cap Spire

El Cap Spire

5.6 chimney

5.12b var

The Ear 5.8 chimney

5.10d Fist

(18)

5.10d or A1

(17)

5.10a

(16)

5.10a

5.9

(15)

5.7 chimney

(14) x

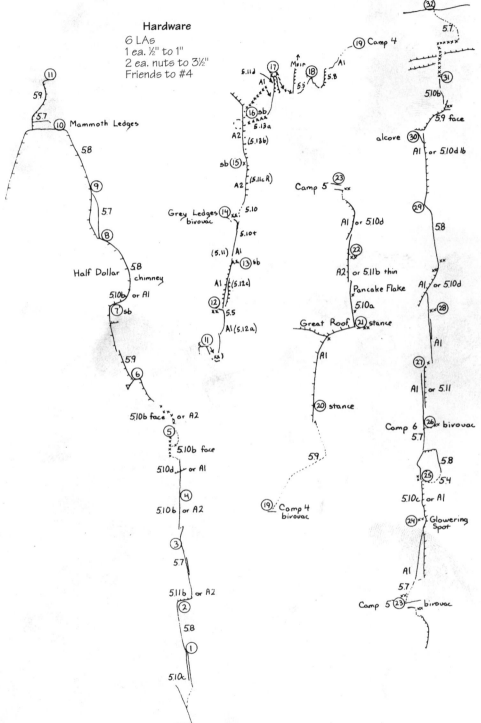

Hardware

6 LAs
1 ea. ½" to 1"
2 ea. nuts to 3½"
Friends to #4

(11)
5.9
5.7
(10) Mammoth Ledges
5.8
(9)
5.7
(8)
5.8 chimney
Half Dollar
5.10b or A1
(7) sb
5.9
(6)
5.10b face or A2
(5)
5.10b face
5.10d or A1
(4)
5.10b or A2
(3)
5.7
5.11b or A2
(2)
5.8
(1)
5.10c

5.11d
A1
(16) sb
5.13a
A2 (5.13b)
sb (15) x
A2 (5.11c R)
Grey Ledges (14) xx 5.10
bivouac
5.10+
(5.11) A1
(13) sb
A1 (5.12d)
(12)
xx 5.5
A1 (5.12a)
(11)
xx

(17)
A1
5.5
Muir
(18)
5.8

(19) Camp 4

Camp 5 (23) xx
A1 or 5.10d
(22)
A2 or 5.11b thin
Pancake Flake
5.10a
Great Roof (21) stance
x
A1
(20) stance

5.9

(19) Camp 4
bivouac

(32)
5.7
x x x x x
(31)
5.10b
xx
5.9 face
alcove (30)
A1 or 5.10d lb
(29)
5.8
xx
A1 or 5.10d
xx (28)
A1
(27) x
A1 or 5.11
(26) xx bivouac
Camp 6
5.7
5.8
(25) 5.4
5.10c or A1
(24) xx Glowering Spot
A1
5.7
Camp 5 (23) xx bivouac

Grape Race
VI 5.9 A4

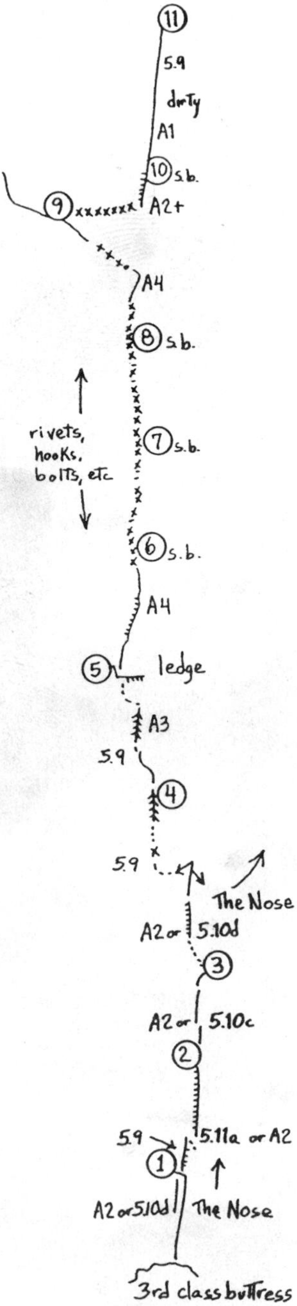

5.9
dirty
A1
10 s.b.
9
A2+
A4
8 s.b.
rivets, hooks, bolts, etc
7 s.b.
6 s.b.
A4
5 ledge
A3
5.9
4
5.9
The Nose
A2 or 5.10d
3
A2 or 5.10c
2
5.9
5.11a or A2
1
A2 or 5.10d
The Nose
3rd class buttress

Hardware

Many hooks, 5 KBs, some pins to 1", heads, in addition to a rack from **The Nose** (see page 69).

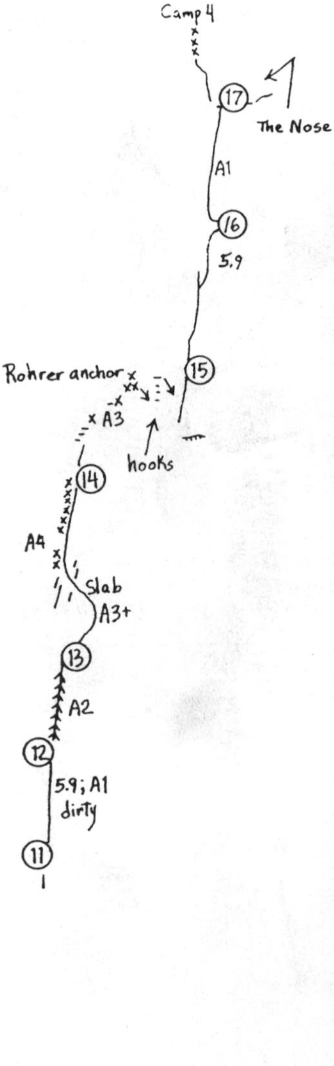

Camp 4
17
The Nose
A1
16
5.9
15
Rohrer anchor
A3
hooks
14
A4
Slab
A3+
13
A2
12
5.9; A1
dirty
11

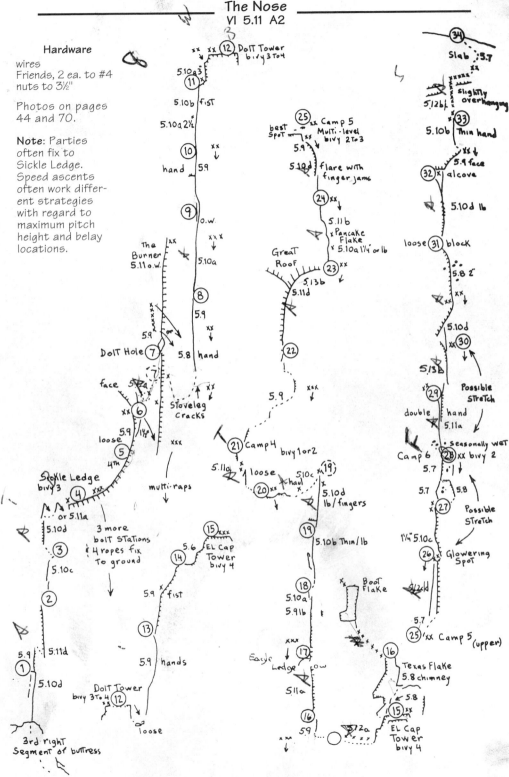

El Capitan:
Southeast Face

20. The Nose
21. New Dawn
22. Pacific Ocean Wall
23. North America Wall

24. New Jersey Turnpike
25. Tangerine Trip
26. Zodiac
27. Eagle's Way

(Note: Arrow on right margin indicates *East Ledges Descent*.
Topo on page 109.)

28. Genesis
29. Mescalito
30. Sea of Dreams
31. Native Son
32. Born Under a Bad Sign
33. Waterfall Route

The Real Nose
VI 5.10 A4

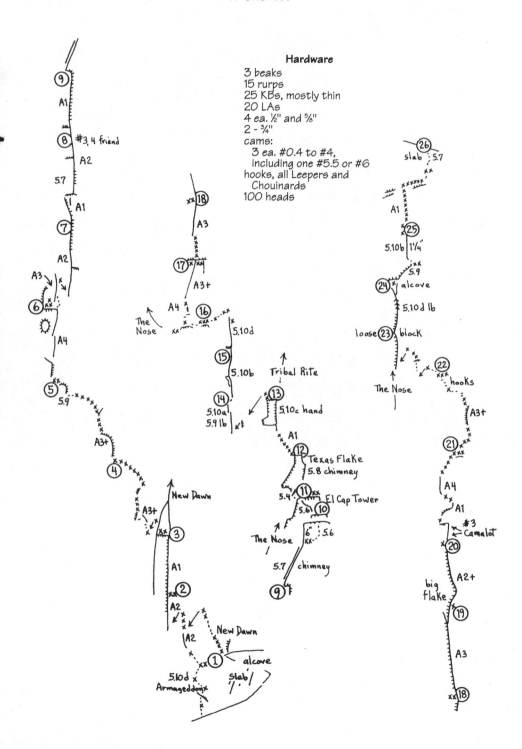

Hardware

3 beaks
15 rurps
25 KBs, mostly thin
20 LAs
4 ea. ½" and ⅝"
2 - ¾"
cams:
   3 ea. #0.4 to #4,
   including one #5.5 or #6
hooks, all Leepers and
   Chouinards
100 heads

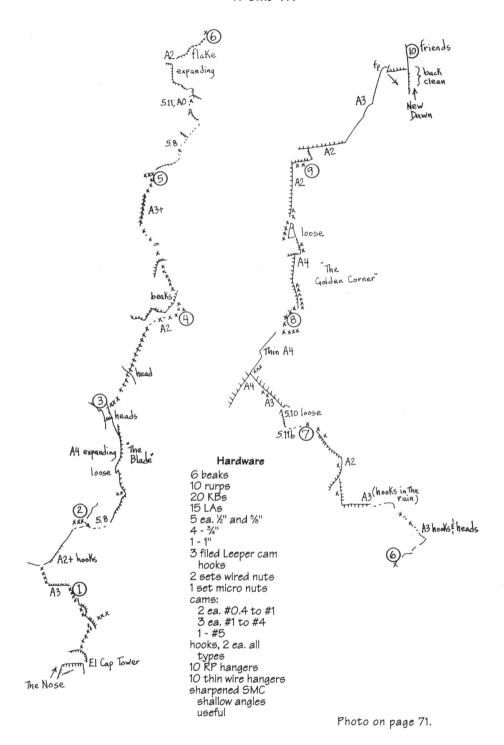

Hardware

6 beaks
10 rurps
20 KBs
15 LAs
5 ea. ½" and ⅝"
4 - ¾"
1 - 1"
3 filed Leeper cam
  hooks
2 sets wired nuts
1 set micro nuts
cams:
  2 ea. #0.4 to #1
  3 ea. #1 to #4
  1 - #5
hooks, 2 ea. all
  types
10 RP hangers
10 thin wire hangers
sharpened SMC
  shallow angles
  useful

Photo on page 71.

Photo on page 70.

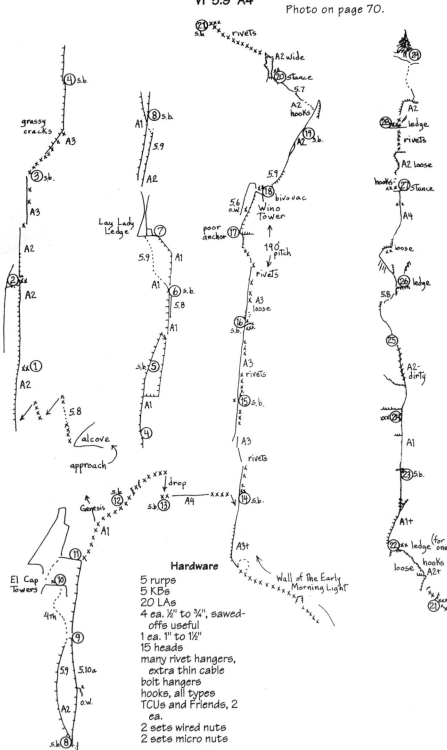

21 s.b. ×××× rivets ××××××××

A2 wide

20 stance
5.7

A2 hooks

19 A2 s.b.

5.9

18 bivouac

5.6 o.w. Wino Tower

poor anchor 17

190' pitch

rivets

A3 loose

16 s.b.

A3 rivets

15 s.b.

A3

rivets

drop

12 s.b. Genesis ×××××× 13 s.b. A4 ×××××× 14 s.b.

A1

11

A3+

Wall of the Early Morning Light

4 s.b.

grassy cracks

A3

3 s.b.

A3

A2

2

A2

1

A2

5.8

alcove

approach

8 s.b.

A1

5.9

A2

Lay Lady Ledge 7

5.9 A1

A1

6 s.b.

5.8

A1

s.b. 5

A1

4

El Cap Towers

10

4th

9

5.9 5.10a

o.w.

A2

s.b. 8

29

A2

28 ledge

rivets

A2 loose

hooks 27 stance

A4

loose

26 ledge

5.8

25

A2- dirty

24

A1

23 s.b.

A1+

22 ledge (for one)

loose hooks A2+

21

Hardware

5 rurps
5 KBs
20 LAs
4 ea. ½" to ¾", sawed-
    offs useful
1 ea. 1" to 1½"
15 heads
many rivet hangers,
    extra thin cable
bolt hangers
hooks, all types
TCUs and Friends, 2
    ea.
2 sets wired nuts
2 sets micro nuts

Mescalito
VI 5.9 A4

Photo on page 71.

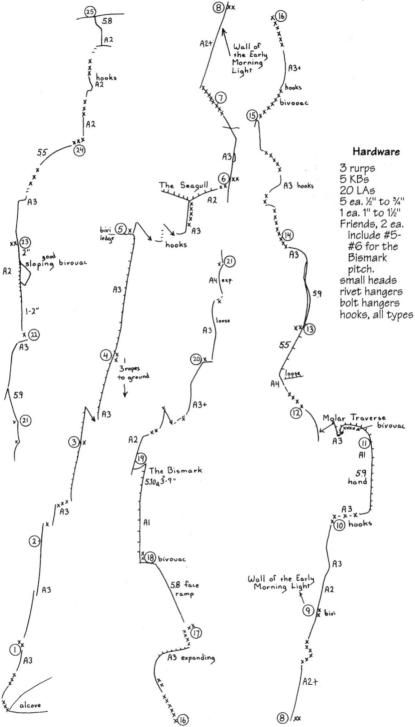

25 5.8

A2

hooks
A2

A2

55 24

A3

xx 23
2"
good
sloping bivouac
A2

1-2"

x 22
A3

5.9

x 21

3 x

xxx
A3

2

A3

1 A3

x alcove

8 xx

A2+

Wall of
the Early
Morning
Light

7

A3

The Seagull
6 xx
A2
hooks
A3

bivi 5 x
ledge

A3

4 x 1
3 ropes
to ground

A2

20

A3+

19
The Bismark
5.10a 3-9"

A1

18 bivouac

5.8 face
ramp

17
A3 expanding

16

16
x
x
x
x
A3+

hooks
bivouac

15

A3 hooks

14
A3

59

x 13
55
loose
A4

12 Molar Traverse
x bivouac
A3 11
A1

5.9
hand

A3
x - x - x
10 hooks

A3

Wall of the Early
Morning Light A2

9 x bivi

A2+

8 xx

21
A4 exp.

x
loose

A3

Hardware

3 rurps
5 KBs
20 LAs
5 ea. ½" to ¾"
1 ea. 1" to 1½"
Friends, 2 ea.
  include #5-
  #6 for the
  Bismark
  pitch.
small heads
rivet hangers
bolt hangers
hooks, all types

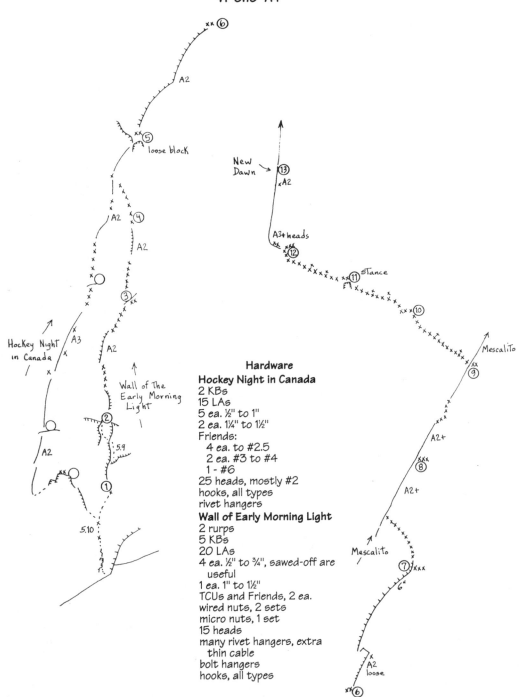

Hockey Night in Canada
VI 5.10 A3
Wall of the Early Morning Light
VI 5.10 A4

xx ⑥

A2

xx ⑤ loose block

A2 ④

A2

③

Hockey Night in Canada — A3

Wall of The Early Morning Light

A2

②

A2 ①

5.9

5.10

New Dawn → ⑬ xA2

A3 + heads
xx ⑫

xx ⑪ stance

xx ⑩

Mescalito
xx ⑨

A2+
xxx ⑧

A2+

Mescalito ⑦ xxx
6"

A2 loose
xx ⑥

Hardware
Hockey Night in Canada
2 KBs
15 LAs
5 ea. ½" to 1"
2 ea. 1¼" to 1½"
Friends:
  4 ea. to #2.5
  2 ea. #3 to #4
  1 - #6
25 heads, mostly #2
hooks, all types
rivet hangers
Wall of Early Morning Light
2 rurps
5 KBs
20 LAs
4 ea. ½" to ¾", sawed-off are
  useful
1 ea. 1" to 1½"
TCUs and Friends, 2 ea.
wired nuts, 2 sets
micro nuts, 1 set
15 heads
many rivet hangers, extra
  thin cable
bolt hangers
hooks, all types

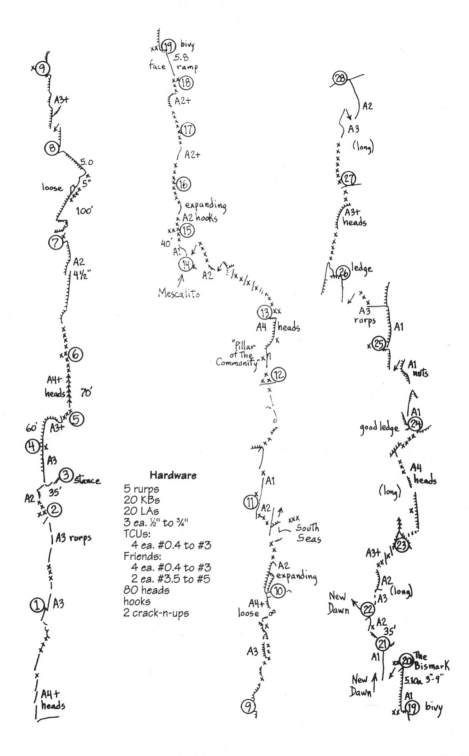

Hardware

5 rurps
20 KBs
20 LAs
3 ea. ½" to ¾"
TCUs:
   4 ea. #0.4 to #3
Friends:
   4 ea. #0.4 to #3
   2 ea. #3.5 to #5
80 heads
hooks
2 crack-n-ups

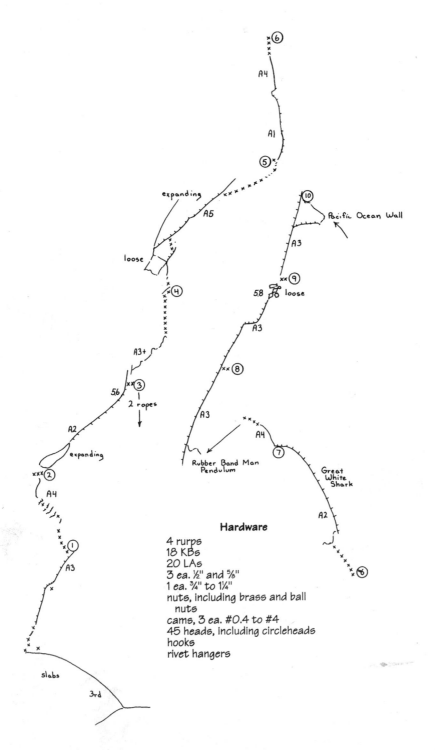

Hardware

4 rurps
18 KBs
20 LAs
3 ea. ½" and ⅝"
1 ea. ¾" to 1¼"
nuts, including brass and ball
   nuts
cams, 3 ea. #0.4 to #4
45 heads, including circleheads
hooks
rivet hangers

Photo on page 70.

Hardware

5 rurps
10 KBs
18 LAs
5 ea. ½" and ⅝"
3 ea. ¾" to 1"
1 ea. 1¼" to 1½"
Friends, 3 ea.
35 heads, mostly small
hooks

Note: This route is closed to climbing from January 1 to August 1 to protect peregrine falcon nesting sites.

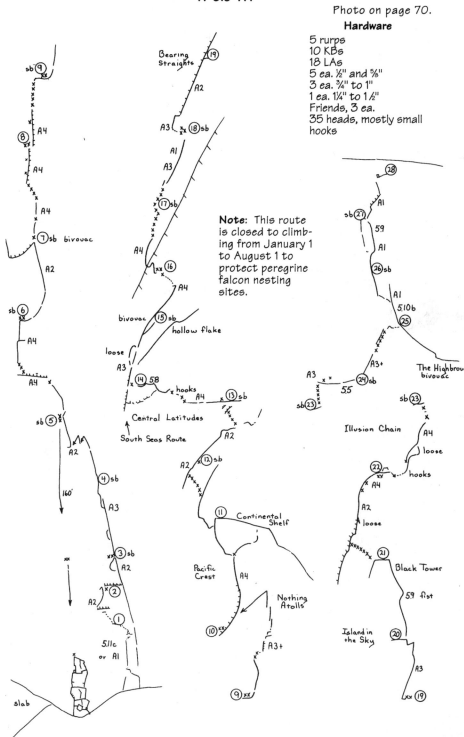

Photo on page 71.

12 exp. anchor
A1
rurp
A4+
11
xx
A5

A4

Continental Shelf
A5 10
9
Hook or Book
5.10 ow 9
bivy
5.9
Easy Street
A3+
8 xx loose
A4
165 ft
A2
7
A2
A5 loose
Laura Scudders flake
6
5 A4 A3
A4
xx 4
hooks
A4
3
A3+
2 xx
A4 hooks
A4 head Var.
A4
1
A3+

23 xx
A4

22 xx

A4
21
A3+ hooks
xx Peruvian Flakes
Cyclops Eye
Sheep A4
Ranch
20 xx Sheep Ranch
A4 bad bolt
hooks
19
A2 9-5 Pitch
Price is Light variation
A3+
A2
18 Bull Dike
rotten
A4
Ace in Space
17
A4 A4
16
A3+
Blue Room
A2
15
To the Tooth A3
xx 14
A4
xx
5.8
Big Sur 13
5.9 ow
Don't Skate Mate
A5 hooks
12

26
5.7
A2
A2+
xx 25
A2
5.8
A1
24
The Igloo
5.8
NA Wall
xx 23

Hardware

5 rurps
20 KBs
25 LAs
5 ea. ½" to ¾"
3 ea. 1" to 1½"
wires
Friends, 4 ea.
100+ heads
hooks, all types

Note: This route is closed to climbing from January 1 to August 1 to protect peregrine falcon nesting sites.

Photo on page 70.

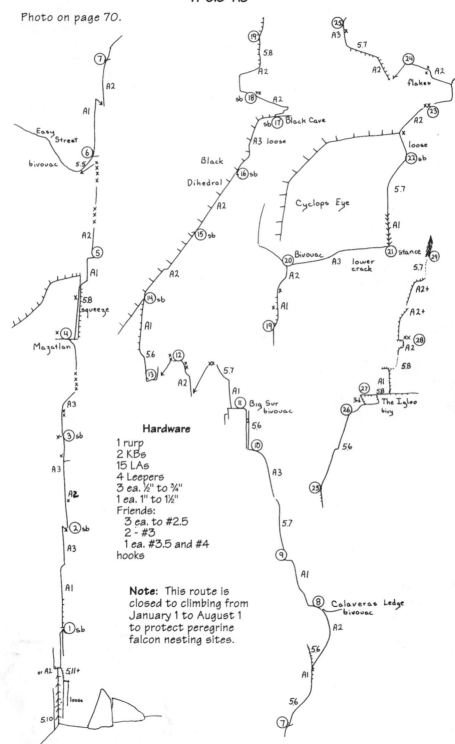

Hardware

1 rurp
2 KBs
15 LAs
4 Leepers
3 ea. ½" to ¾"
1 ea. 1" to 1½"
Friends:
 3 ea. to #2.5
 2 - #3
 1 ea. #3.5 and #4
hooks

Note: This route is closed to climbing from January 1 to August 1 to protect peregrine falcon nesting sites.

Note: This route is closed to climbing from January 1 to August 1 to protect peregrine falcon nesting sites.

Hardware

5 rurps
35 KBs
25 LAs
5 ea. ½" to 1¼"
Friends, 4 ea.
wires
100 heads
hooks, all types

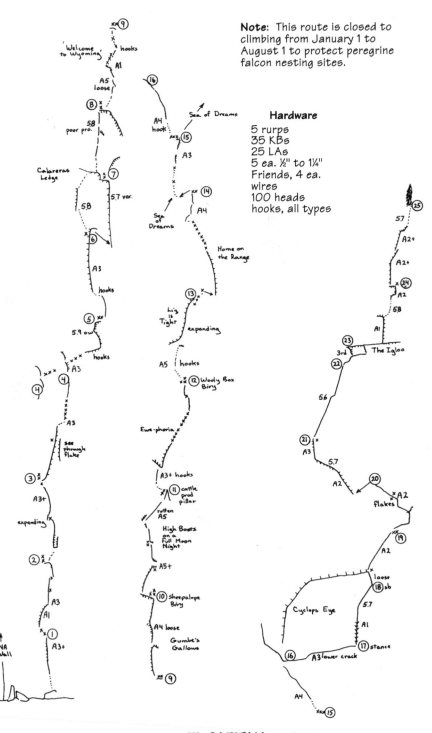

'Welcome to Wyoming'
hooks
A1
A5 loose
⑧
58 poor pro.
Calaveras Ledge
⑦
5.7 var.
58
⑥
A3
hooks
⑤
5.9 ow
hooks
A3
④
④
A3
see through flake
③
A3+
expanding
②
A3
A1
①
A3+
NA Wall
⑨
Sea of Dreams
⑯
A4 hook
⑮
A3
⑭
A4
Sea of Dreams
Home on the Range
⑬
Li's Tight
expanding
A5 hooks
⑫ Wooly Box Bivy
Ewe-phoria
A3+ hooks
⑪ cattle prod pillar
rotten A5
High Boots on a Full Moon Night
A5+
⑩ Sheepalope Bivy
A4 loose
Gumbe's Gallows
⑨
⑮
57
A2+
A2+
⑭
A2
58
A1
⑮
3rd
⑮ The Igloo
⑫
56
⑪
A3
5.7
A2
⑳
A2
Flakes
⑲
A2
loose
⑱ ab
5.7
A1
⑰ stance
Cyclops Eye
⑯
A3 lower crack
A4
⑮

Hardware

20 KBs
20 LAs
4 ea. ½" to ¾"
2 - 1"
1 ea. 1¼" to 1½"
wires
TCUs
Friends:
 3 ea. #1 to #3
 1 - #4
65 heads, including 5 circleheads
hooks, all types
RP (keyhole) hangers

Note: This route is closed to climbing from January 1 to August 1 to protect peregrine falcon nesting sites.

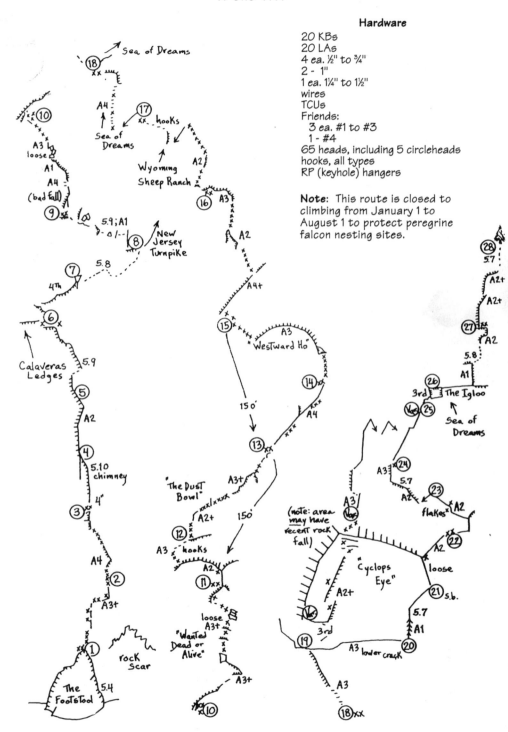

Photo on page 70.

Hardware

5 rurps
10 KBs
25 LAs
6 ea. ½" and ⅝"
5 - ¾", including sawed-off
2 - 1"
1 - 1¼"
50 heads, mostly #1s and
    #2s

⑨ xx | bolts on bad rock

5.10c
Steep loose flakes

⑧

⑦ 5.8
4ᵗʰ

⑥

Calaveras Ledges 5.9

⑤

A2

④

5.10 chimney

4"
③ xx

A4

② xx
A3+

xx ① The Footstool 5.4

rock Scar

Note: This route is closed to climbing from January 1 to August 1 to protect peregrine falcon nesting sites.

good ledge ⑲ xx
A3+

Sloping ledge ⑱

5.9
A1

⑯ A3 xx
30' A2
⑰

⑮ xx
A3

⑭ xx
A2

Iron Hawk

A2
⑬
⑫ 5.9
5.10

⑪
Atlantic Ocean Wall

A4

xx ⑩

x A4+

xx ⑨

㉓
5.7 30'
㉒

A3

㉑

5.9

⑳ xx
5.9

xx dike

⑲ xx

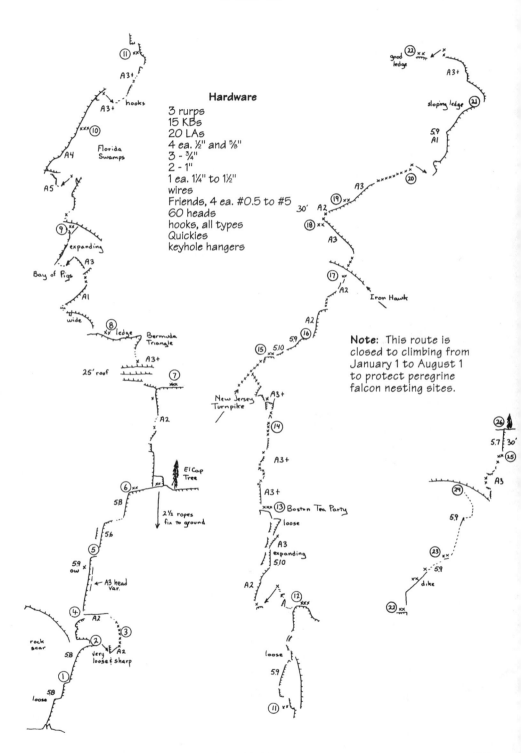

Hardware

3 rurps
15 KBs
20 LAs
4 ea. ½" and ⅝"
3 - ¾"
2 - 1"
1 ea. 1¼" to 1½"
wires
Friends, 4 ea. #0.5 to #5
60 heads
hooks, all types
Quickies
keyhole hangers

Note: This route is closed to climbing from January 1 to August 1 to protect peregrine falcon nesting sites.

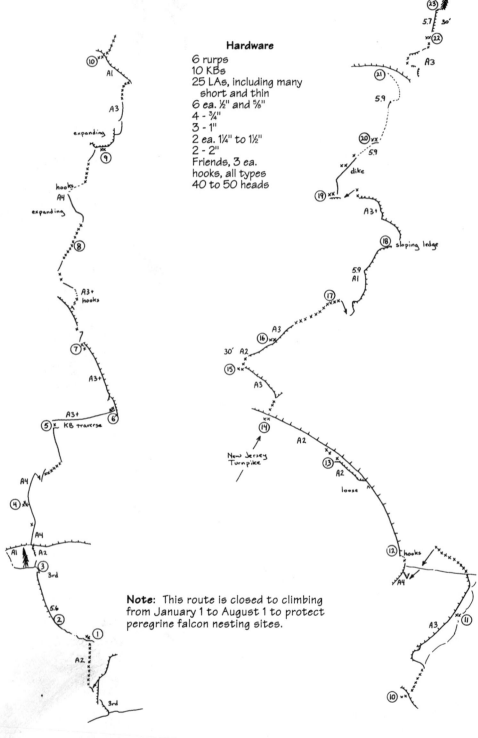

Hardware

6 rurps
10 KBs
25 LAs, including many
  short and thin
6 ea. ½" and ⅝"
4 - ¾"
3 - 1"
2 ea. 1¼" to 1½"
2 - 2"
Friends, 3 ea.
hooks, all types
40 to 50 heads

Note: This route is closed to climbing
from January 1 to August 1 to protect
peregrine falcon nesting sites.

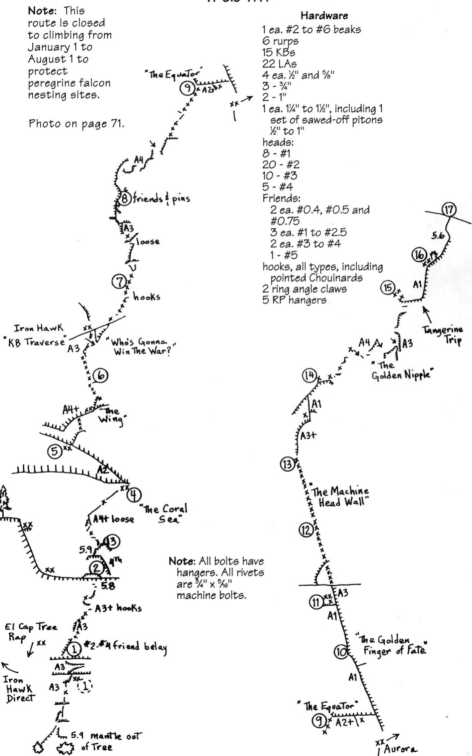

Note: This route is closed to climbing from January 1 to August 1 to protect peregrine falcon nesting sites.

Photo on page 71.

Hardware

1 ea. #2 to #6 beaks
6 rurps
15 KBs
22 LAs
4 ea. ½" and ⅝"
3 - ¾"
2 - 1"
1 ea. 1¼" to 1½", including 1
   set of sawed-off pitons
   ½" to 1"
heads:
8 - #1
20 - #2
10 - #3
5 - #4
Friends:
   2 ea. #0.4, #0.5 and
   #0.75
   3 ea. #1 to #2.5
   2 ea. #3 to #4
   1 - #5
hooks, all types, including
   pointed Chouinards
2 ring angle claws
5 RP hangers

"The Equator"
⑨ A2½
A4
⑧ friends & pins
A3
loose
⑦
hooks
Iron Hawk
"KB Traverse"
A3
"Who's Gonna
Win The War?"
⑥
A4+
"The Wing"
⑤
A2
④
"The Coral Sea"
A4+ loose
5.9 ③
4th
②
- 5.8
- A3+ hooks
El Cap Tree Rap
A3
① #2-#4 friend belay
A3
A3 (1)
Iron Hawk Direct
5.9 mantle out of Tree

Note: All bolts have hangers. All rivets are ¾" x ⁵⁄₁₆" machine bolts.

⑰
5.6
⑯
⑮ A1
Tangerine Trip
A4 A3
"The Golden Nipple"
⑭
A1
A3+
⑬
"The Machine Head Wall"
⑫
⑪ A3
A1
"The Golden Finger of Fate"
⑩
A1
"The Equator"
⑨ A2+
Aurora

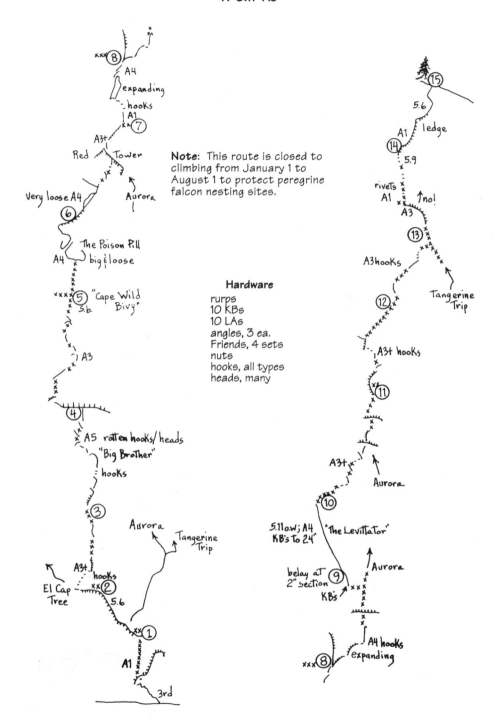

Note: This route is closed to climbing from January 1 to August 1 to protect peregrine falcon nesting sites.

Hardware

rurps
10 KBs
10 LAs
angles, 3 ea.
Friends, 4 sets
nuts
hooks, all types
heads, many

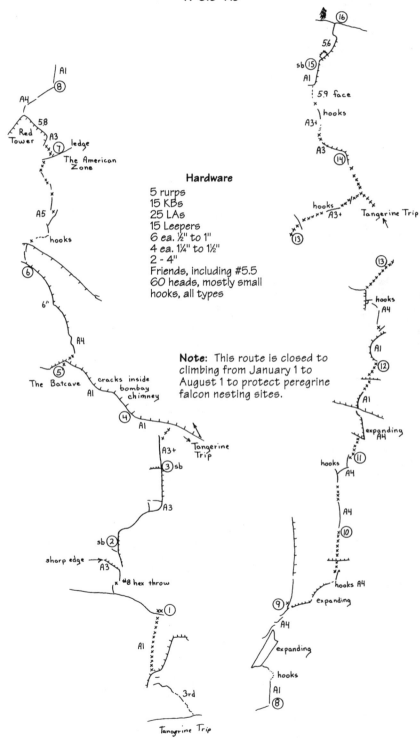

16

56

sb 15
A1

5.9 face
hooks
A3+

A3
14

hooks
A3+   Tangerine Trip

13

13

hooks
A4

A1
12

A1

expanding
A4

hooks
11
A4

A4

10

hooks A4
9   expanding
A4

expanding

hooks
A1
8

A1
8

A4
Red
Tower   58
A3   ledge
7
The American
Zone

A5
hooks

6
6"

A4

5
The Batcave   cracks inside
A1   bombay
chimney
4   A1
A3+   Tangerine
Trip
3 sb
A3
sb 2
sharp edge
A3
#8 hex throw
xx 1
A1
3rd
Tangerine Trip

Hardware

5 rurps
15 KBs
25 LAs
15 Leepers
6 ea. ½" to 1"
4 ea. 1¼" to 1½"
2 - 4"
Friends, including #5.5
60 heads, mostly small
hooks, all types

Note: This route is closed to climbing from January 1 to August 1 to protect peregrine falcon nesting sites.

Photo on page 70.

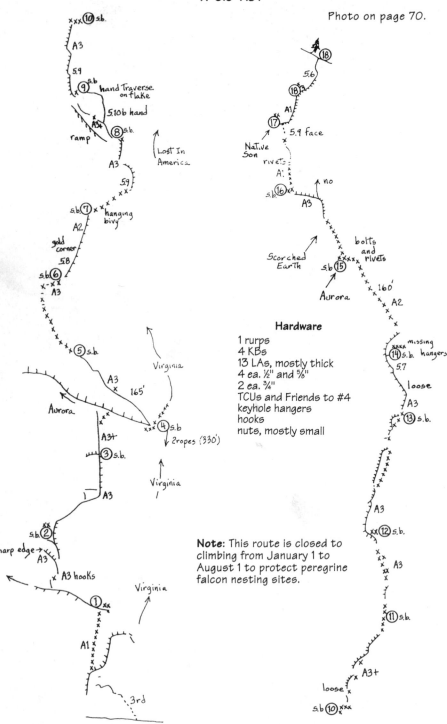

Hardware

1 rurps
4 KBs
13 LAs, mostly thick
4 ea. ½" and ⅝"
2 ea. ¾"
TCUs and Friends to #4
keyhole hangers
hooks
nuts, mostly small

Note: This route is closed to climbing from January 1 to August 1 to protect peregrine falcon nesting sites.

Third pitch of the **North America Wall** during the first ascent in 1964. Photo: Tom Frost.

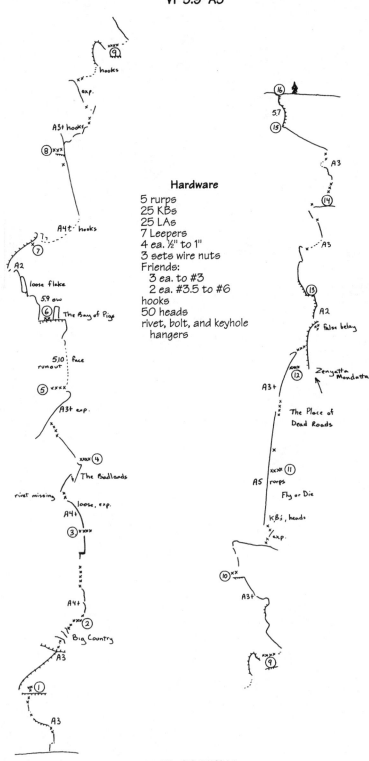

Hardware

5 rurps
25 KBs
25 LAs
7 Leepers
4 ea. ½" to 1"
3 sets wire nuts
Friends:
  3 ea. to #3
  2 ea. #3.5 to #6
hooks
50 heads
rivet, bolt, and keyhole
  hangers

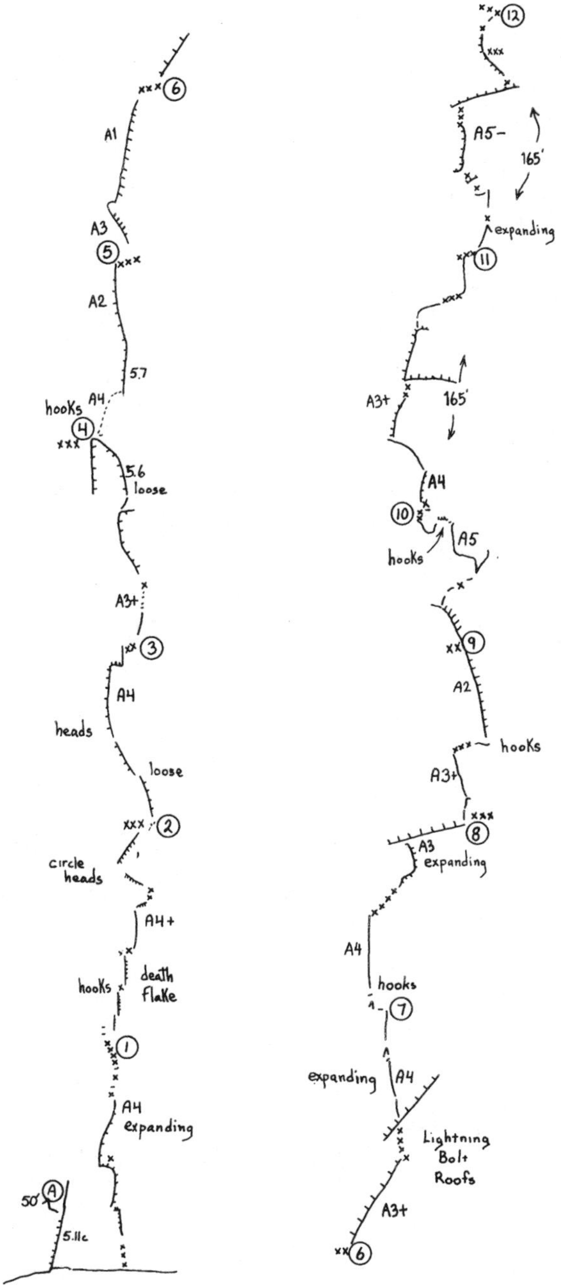

Hardware

5 rurps
20 KBs
15 LAs
4 ea. ½" and ⅝"
2 ea. ¾" to 1"
hooks, all types including
  pointed Chouinards
50 heads:
  5 - #1
  30 - #2
  10 - #3
  5 - #4
cams:
  2 ea. to #3
  1 ea. #3.5 to #4

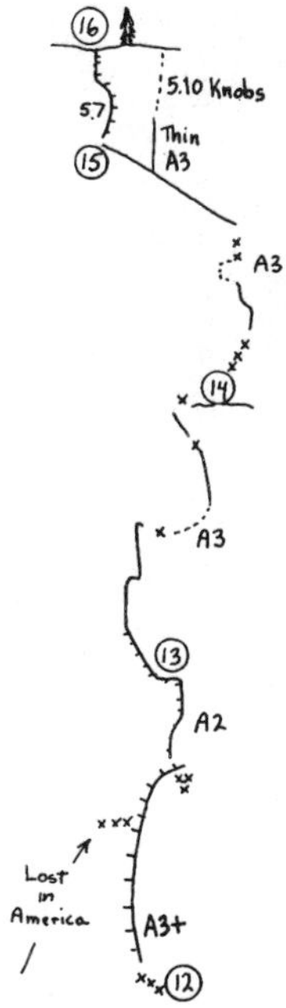

⑥ A1

A3
⑤ xxx
A2

5.7
hooks A4
④ xxx
5.6
loose

A3+ x
③
A4
heads
loose
xxx ②
circle
heads
A4+
hooks death
flake
①
A4
expanding
50' Ⓐ
5.11c

⑫ xxx
A5−
165'
expanding
⑪
A3+ 165'
A4
⑩
hooks A5
⑨ xx
A2
hooks
A3+
⑧ xxx
A3
expanding
A4
hooks
⑦
expanding A4
Lightning
Bolt
Roofs
A3+
xx ⑥

⑯
5.10 Knobs
5.7 Thin
⑮ A3
A3
⑭ x
A3
⑬
A2
Lost
in xxx
America A3+
xxx ⑫

The Shortest Straw
VI 5.10 A3+

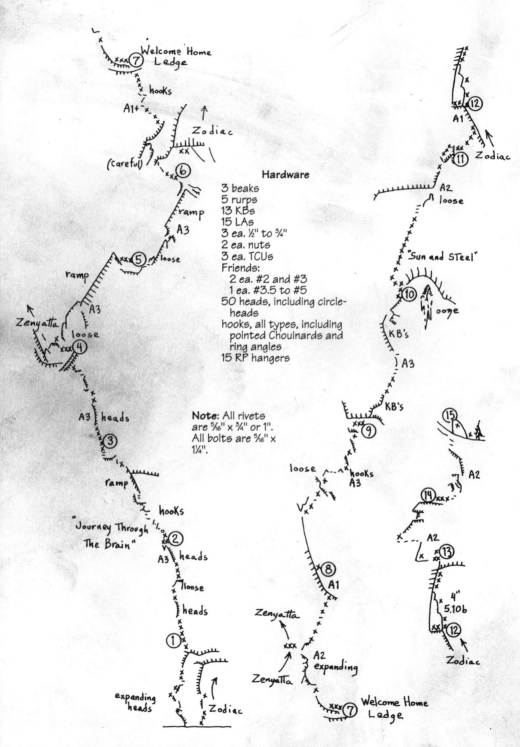

Welcome Home Ledge
⑦
hooks
A1+
Zodiac
(careful)
⑥
ramp
A3
ramp
⑤ loose
A3
Zenyatta
loose
④
A3 heads
③
ramp
hooks
"Journey Through The Brain"
②
A3 heads
loose
heads
①
expanding heads
Zodiac

Hardware

3 beaks
5 rurps
13 KBs
15 LAs
3 ea. ½" to ¾"
2 ea. nuts
3 ea. TCUs
Friends:
  2 ea. #2 and #3
  1 ea. #3.5 to #5
50 heads, including circleheads
hooks, all types, including
  pointed Chouinards and
  ring angles
15 RP hangers

Note: All rivets
are ⁵⁄₁₆" x ¾" or 1".
All bolts are ⁵⁄₁₆" x
1¼".

⑫
A1
Zodiac
⑪
A2
loose
"Sun and Steel"
⑩
ooze
KB's
A3
KB's
⑨
loose
hooks
A3
⑮
A2
⑭
A2
⑬
4"
5.10b
⑫
Zodiac

loose
hooks
A3
⑧
A1
Zenyatta
Zenyatta
A2 expanding
Zenyatta
Welcome Home Ledge
⑦

Hardware

3 rurps
4 KBs
15 LAs, mostly short and
   thick
3 ea. ½" to ¾"
1 ea. 1" to 1½"
2 sets wired nuts, including
   brass
10 nuts, ¼" x 20
Friends, 2 ea.
2 sets TCUs
8 heads, mostly small
hooks
10 bolt hangers

Photo on page 70.

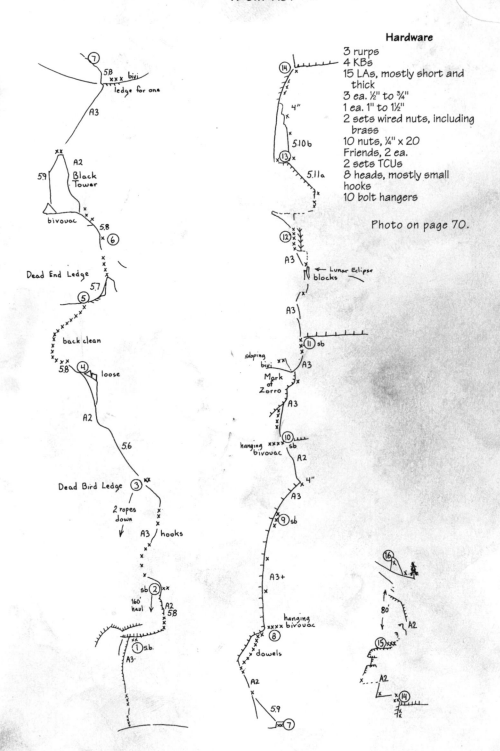

⑦ 5.8
xxx bivi
ledge for one
A3

xx A2
5.9 Black
     Tower
bivouac
5.8
x ⑥
Dead End Ledge
5.7
⑤
back clean
5.8 ④ loose
A2
5.6
Dead Bird Ledge xx
③
2 ropes
down
A3 / hooks
sb ② xx
160' A2
haul 5.8
xx ① s.b.
A3

⑭ x
4" x
5.10b
⑬
5.11a
⑫ xxxx
A3   ← Lunar Eclipse
         blocks
A3
⑪ sb
sloping xx
bivi   A3
Mark
of
Zorro
A3
hanging xxx ⑩
bivouac sb
A2
4"
A3
x ⑨ sb

A3+

hanging
xxxx bivouac
⑧
dowels
A2
5.9
x ⑦

⑯
80'
A2
⑮ xxx
x A2
⑭

Hardware
5 beaks
2 rurps
20 KBs
16 LAs
3 ea. ½" and ⅝"
1 ea. ¾" to 1"
Friends:
  3 ea. #0.4 to #2.5
  2 ea. #3 to #4
60 heads:
  5 - #1
  25 - #2
  20 - #3
  5 - #4
  5 - #5
hooks, all types

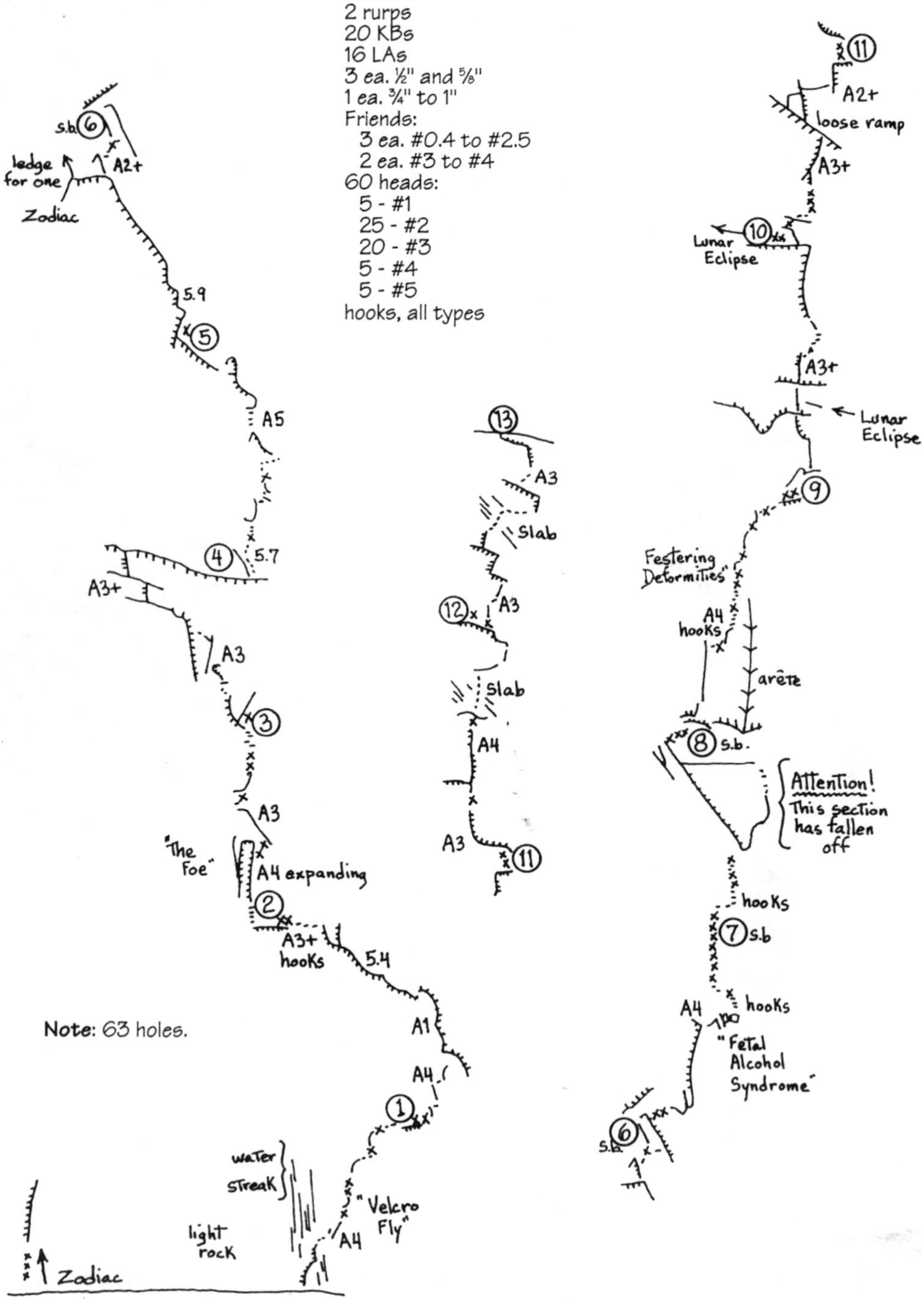

s.b. ⑥
ledge for one
A2+
Zodiac

5.9
⑤

A5

④ 5.7
A3+

A3
③

A3

"The Foe"
A4 expanding
②
A3+ hooks
5.4

Note: 63 holes.

A1

A4
①

water streak
light rock
"Velcro Fly"
A4

↑ Zodiac

⑪
A2+
loose ramp
A3+

⑩
Lunar Eclipse

A3+

← Lunar Eclipse

x ⑨

Festering Deformities

A4 hooks

arête

⑧ s.b.

Attention! This section has fallen off

hooks
⑦ s.b.

A4 hooks
"Fetal Alcohol Syndrome"

s.b. ⑥

⑬
A3
Slab

⑫ x A3

Slab
A4

A3
⑪

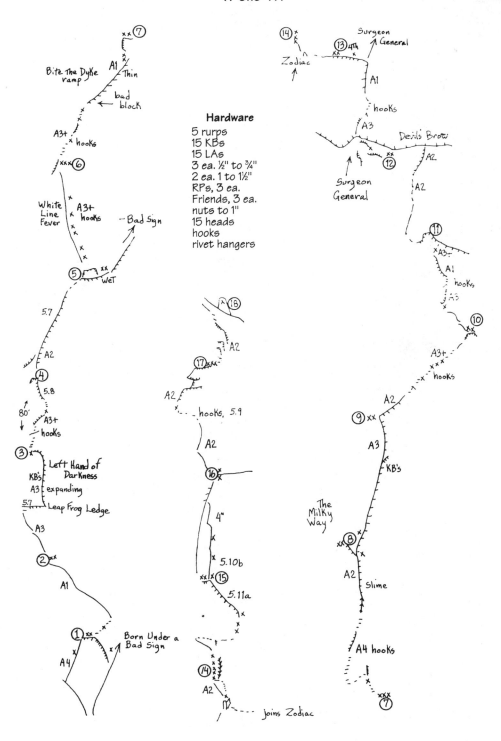

Bite The Dyke ramp

A1 Thin

bad block

A3+ hooks

⑦
⑥

White Line Fever

A3+ hooks

··· Bad Sign

⑤ WeT

5.7

A2

④ 5.8

80'

A3+ hooks

③

Left Hand of Darkness

KB's

A3 expanding

5.7 Leap Frog Ledge

A3

②

A1

① Born Under a Bad Sign

A4

Hardware

5 rurps
15 KBs
15 LAs
3 ea. ½" to ¾"
2 ea. 1 to 1½"
RPs, 3 ea.
Friends, 3 ea.
nuts to 1"
15 heads
hooks
rivet hangers

⑱ A

A2

⑰

A2

hooks, 5.9

A2

⑯

4"

5.10b

⑮ 5.11a

⑭

A2

joins Zodiac

⑭

Zodiac

⑬ 4th

Surgeon General

A1

hooks

A3 Devil's Brow

⑫ A2

Surgeon General

A2

⑪

A3+

A1 hooks

A3

⑩

A3+ hooks

A2

⑨ xx

A3

KB's

The Milky Way

⑧

A2 Slime

A4 hooks

⑦

Photo on page 71.

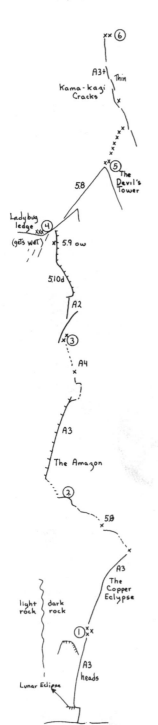

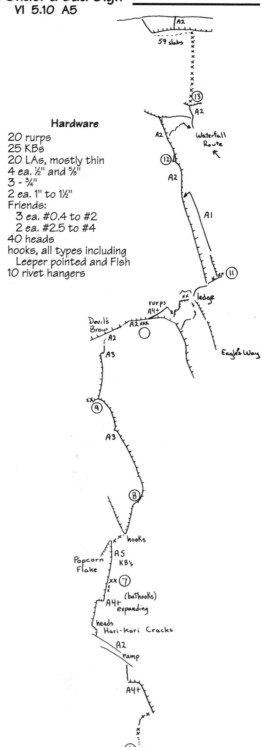

Hardware

20 rurps
25 KBs
20 LAs, mostly thin
4 ea. ½" and ⅝"
3 - ¾"
2 ea. 1" to 1½"
Friends:
 3 ea. #0.4 to #2
 2 ea. #2.5 to #4
40 heads
hooks, all types including
  Leeper pointed and Fish
10 rivet hangers

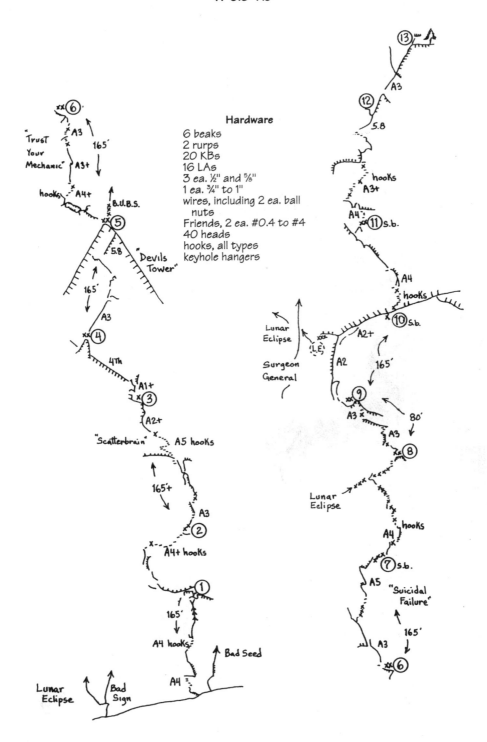

Hardware

6 beaks
2 rurps
20 KBs
16 LAs
3 ea. ½" and ⅝"
1 ea. ¾" to 1"
wires, including 2 ea. ball
    nuts
Friends, 2 ea. #0.4 to #4
40 heads
hooks, all types
keyhole hangers

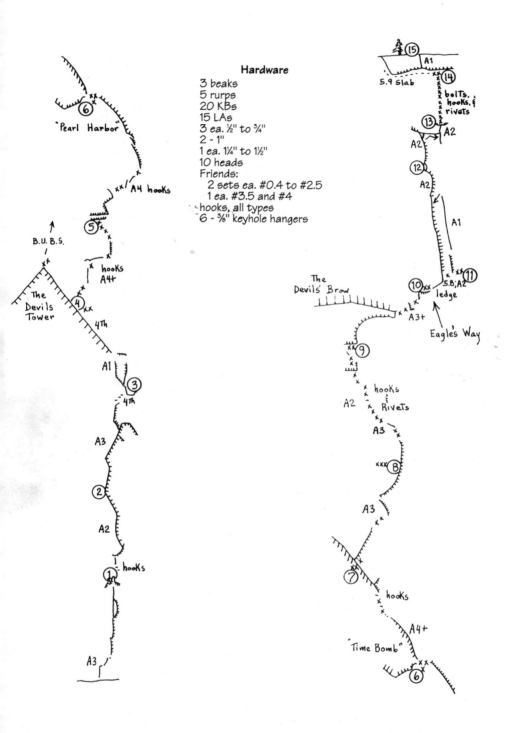

Hardware
3 beaks
5 rurps
20 KBs
15 LAs
3 ea. ½" to ¾"
2 - 1"
1 ea. 1¼" to 1½"
10 heads
Friends:
    2 sets ea. #0.4 to #2.5
    1 ea. #3.5 and #4
hooks, all types
6 - ⅜" keyhole hangers

"Pearl Harbor"

A4 hooks

B.U.B.S.

The
Devils
Tower

The
Devils' Brow

5.9 slab

bolts,
hooks, &
rivets

A2

A2

A1

5.8, A2
ledge

Eagle's Way

A3+

hooks
&
Rivets

A3

A3

hooks

A4+

"Time Bomb"

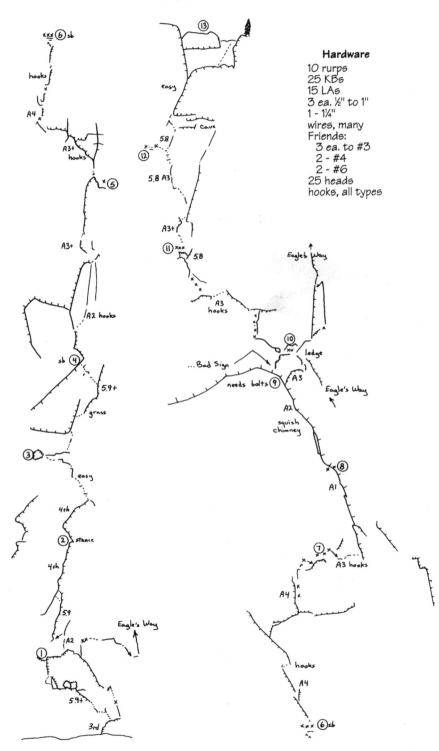

Hardware

10 rurps
25 KBs
15 LAs
3 ea. ½" to 1"
1 - 1¼"
wires, many
Friends:
 3 ea. to #3
 2 - #4
 2 - #6
25 heads
hooks, all types

Eagle's Way
VI 5.10a A4

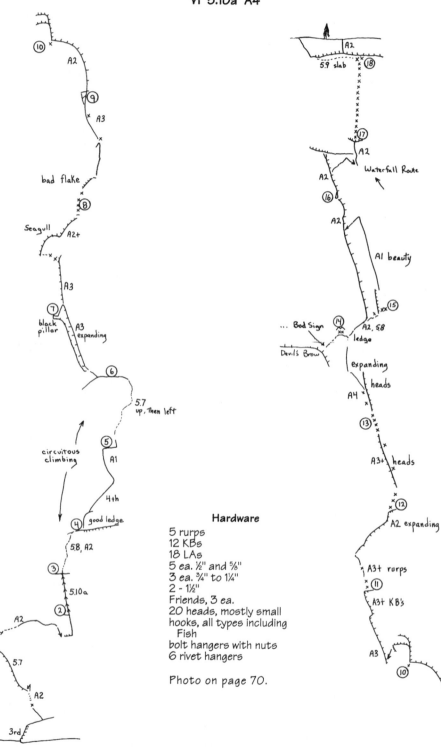

Hardware

5 rurps
12 KBs
18 LAs
5 ea. ½" and ⅝"
3 ea. ¾" to 1¼"
2 - 1½"
Friends, 3 ea.
20 heads, mostly small
hooks, all types including
    Fish
bolt hangers with nuts
6 rivet hangers

Photo on page 70.

On the Waterfront
VI 5.9 A5

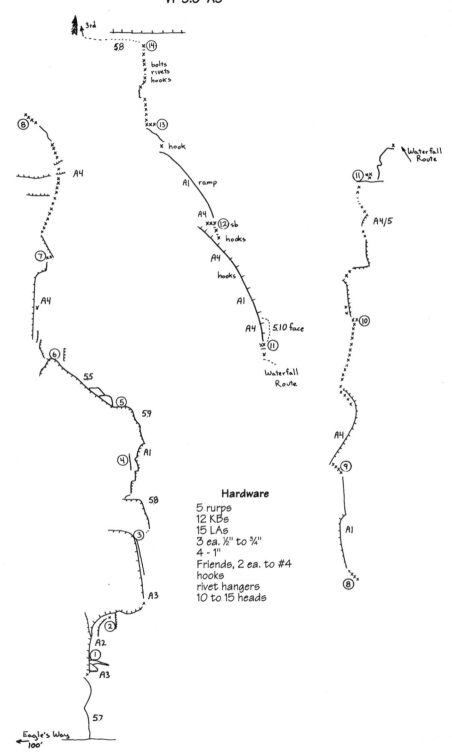

3rd

5.8

⑭

bolts
rivets
hooks

⑬

hook

A1 ramp

A4

⑫ sb

hooks

A4

hooks

A1

A4

5.10 face

⑪

Waterfall
Route

⑧

A4

⑦

A4

⑥

5.5

⑤

5.9

④ A1

5.8

③

A3

②

A2

①

A3

5.7

Eagle's Way
100'

Waterfall
Route

⑪ xx

A4/5

⑩

A4

⑨

A1

⑧

Hardware

5 rurps
12 KBs
15 LAs
3 ea. ½" to ¾"
4 - 1"
Friends, 2 ea. to #4
hooks
rivet hangers
10 to 15 heads

Hardware
1 beak
12 KBs
20 LAs
3 ea. ½" to 1"
nuts, including ball nuts
Friends, 3 ea. #0.4 to #4
50 heads
keyhole hangers

Note: 64 holes.

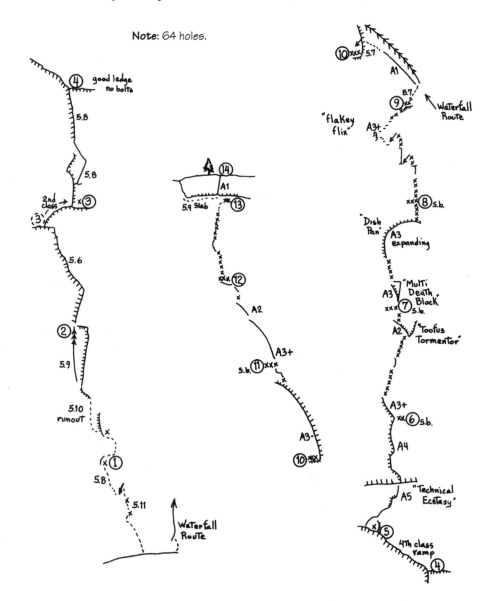

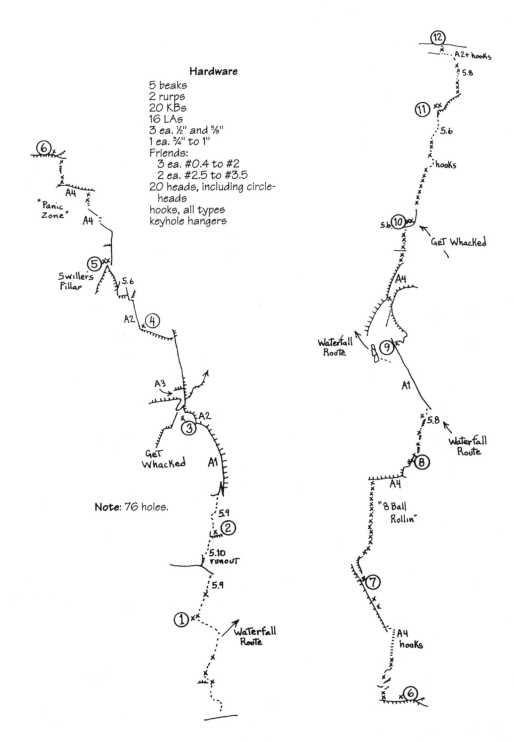

Hardware

5 beaks
2 rurps
20 KBs
16 LAs
3 ea. ½" and ⅝"
1 ea. ¾" to 1"
Friends:
  3 ea. #0.4 to #2
  2 ea. #2.5 to #3.5
20 heads, including circleheads
hooks, all types
keyhole hangers

"Panic Zone"   A4
A4

Swillers Pillar   5.6
5

A2   4

A3
A2   3

Get Whacked   A1

Note: 76 holes.

5.9
2
5.10 runout
5.9
1   Waterfall Route

12   A2+ hooks
5.8
11   5.6
hooks
5.6 10   Get Whacked
A4
Waterfall Route
9
A1
5.8
Waterfall Route
8
A4
"8 Ball Rollin"
7
A4 hooks
6

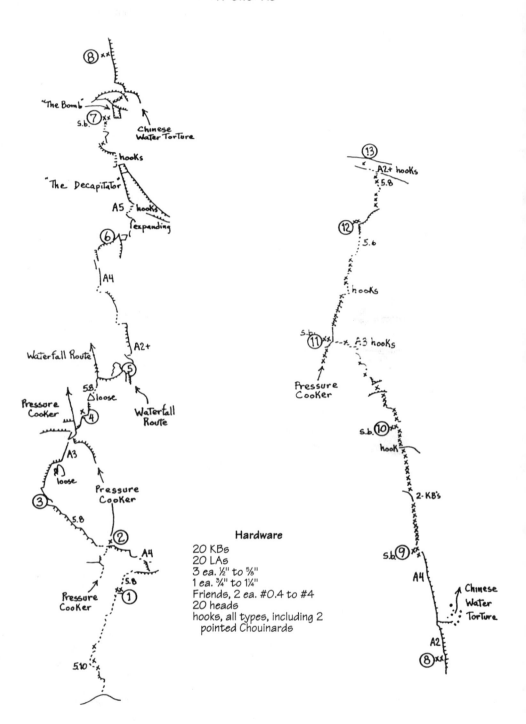

Hardware
20 KBs
20 LAs
3 ea. ½" to ⅝"
1 ea. ¾" to 1¼"
Friends, 2 ea. #0.4 to #4
20 heads
hooks, all types, including 2
   pointed Chouinards

Photo on page 71.

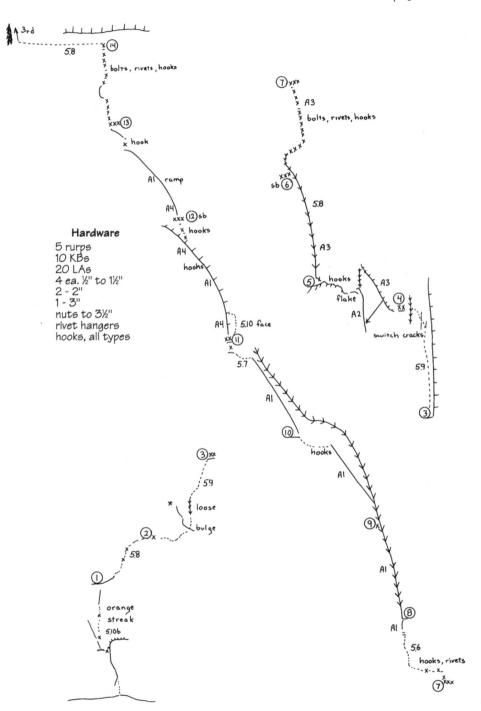

3rd

5.8 ⑭

bolts, rivets, hooks

xxx ⑬

hook

A1 ramp

A4

xxx ⑫ sb

hooks

A4

hooks

A1

A4 5.10 face

xx ⑪
x

5.7

A1

⑩

hooks

A1

⑦ xxx

A3

bolts, rivets, hooks

xxx
sb ⑥

5.8

A3

⑤ hooks

flake

A3

A2

④
xx

switch cracks

5.9

⑨ x

A1

⑧

A1

5.6

hooks, rivets

x - x

⑦ xxx

③ xx

5.9

x loose

bulge

② x

5.8

①

orange
streak

5.10b

Hardware

5 rurps
10 KBs
20 LAs
4 ea. ½" to 1½"
2 - 2"
1 - 3"
nuts to 3½"
rivet hangers
hooks, all types

Hardware

10 rurps
15 KBs
15 LAs
3 ea. ½" and ⅝"
2 - ¾"
1 ea. 1¼" to 1½"
Friends, 4 ea.
wires, many small
30 heads, mostly
  small
hooks, all types

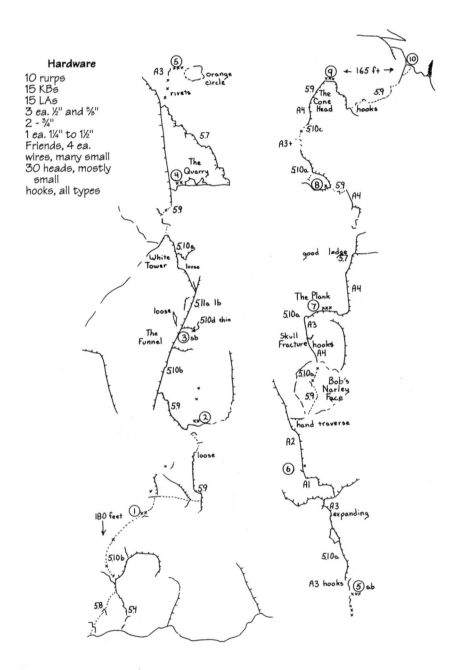

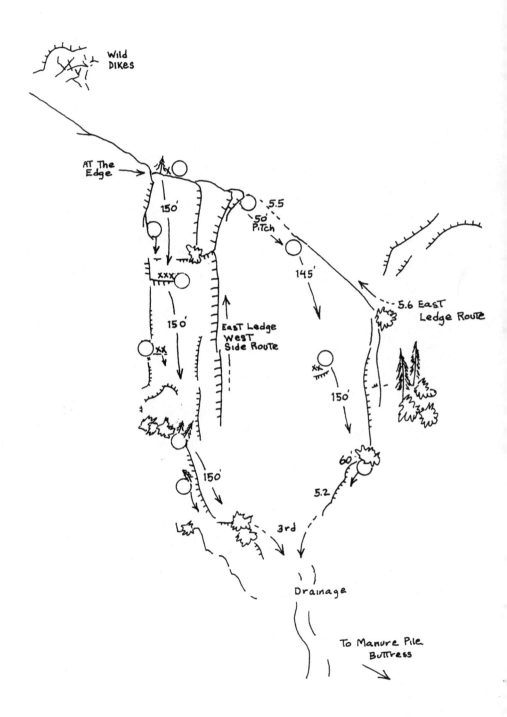

Wild DIKES

AT The Edge →

150'

5.5

50' Pitch

5.6 East Ledge Route

145'

XXX

150'

East Ledge West Side Route

XX

150'

150'

60'

150'

5.2

3rd

Drainage

To Manure Pile Buttress

Via Aqua

off

Upper Yosemite Falls

1. Wheel of Torture
2. World of Pain
3. Via sin Liquor
4. Misty Wall
5. Aqua Vulva

6. Dante's Inferno
7. Lost Arrow Spire, Direct Route
8. Yosemite Pointless
9. Czech Route

Approach: To get to the base of the upper wall it is necessary to gain the top of Sunnyside Bench, the lowest and most prominent wooded tier right of Yosemite Falls. Either climb the Sunnyside Bench (5.0) route (not provided) or a talus field directly behind the Park Service maintenance yard and fire station. At a point overlooking the lip of Lower Yosemite Fall, a tiny section of 3rd class begins a right diagonalling wooded ramp. Class 3 friction off the ramp leads to the 2nd tier. The final section involves a march through oaks and manzanita before sandy slopes lead to the base of the Lost Arrow.

Photo on page 110.

Pitch	Rivets	Bolts	Total
1	0	1	1
2	4	2	6
3	7	2	9
4	4	2	6
5	10	2	12
6	0	2	2
7	0	1	1
8	6	2	8
9	0	2	2
10	1	0	1
Total	32	16	48

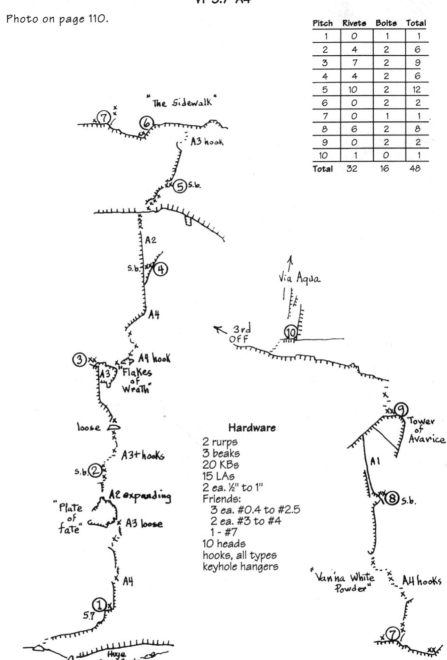

"The Sidewalk"

⑦ ⑥

A3 hook

⑤ s.b.

A2

s.b. ④

A4

③ A4 hook

A3 "Flakes of Wrath"

loose

A3+ hooks

s.b. ②

A2 expanding

"Plate of fate"

A3 loose

A4

① 5.7

Huge Cave

Via Aqua

← 3rd OFF

⑩

× ⑨ Tower of Avarice

A1

⑧ s.b.

"Van'na White Powder"   A4 hooks

⑦

Hardware
2 rurps
3 beaks
20 KBs
15 LAs
2 ea. ½" to 1"
Friends:
  3 ea. #0.4 to #2.5
  2 ea. #3 to #4
  1 - #7
10 heads
hooks, all types
keyhole hangers

World of Pain
VI 5.8 A5

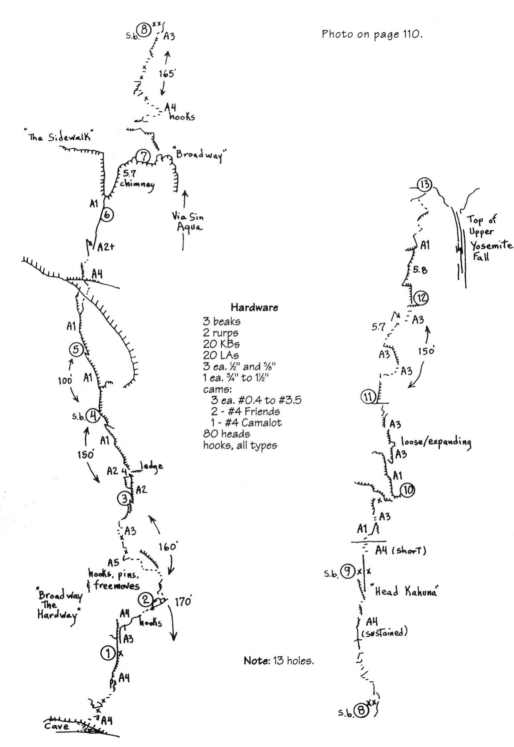

Photo on page 110.

Hardware

3 beaks
2 rurps
20 KBs
20 LAs
3 ea. ½" and ⅝"
1 ea. ¾" to 1½"
cams:
   3 ea. #0.4 to #3.5
   2 - #4 Friends
   1 - #4 Camalot
80 heads
hooks, all types

Note: 13 holes.

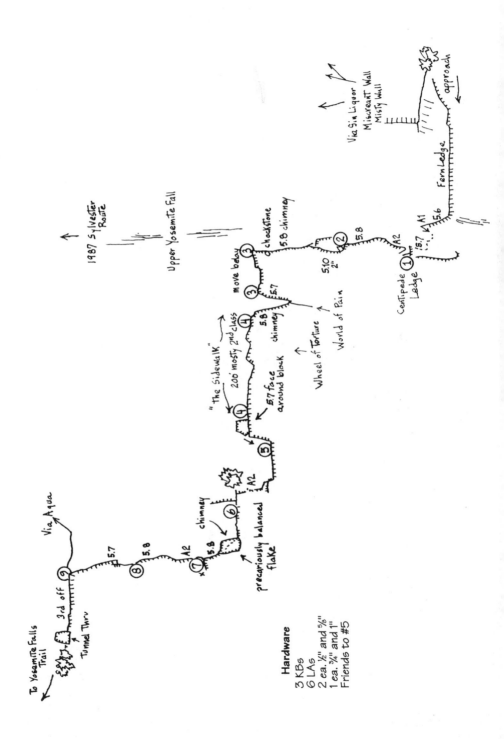

Via sin Liquor
VI 5.9 A4
Miscreant Wall
V 5.9 A4
Misty Wall
V 5.11d A0

Photo on page 110.

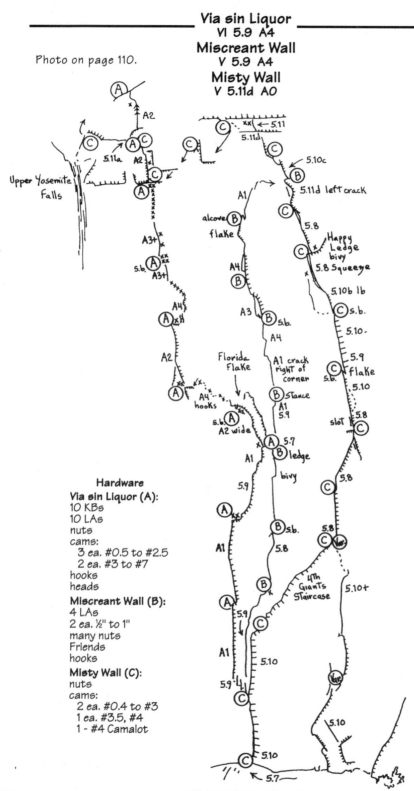

A2

Upper Yosemite Falls

5.11a   A2

A3+

s.b.   A3+

A4

A2

A4 hooks

A2 wide

A1

5.9

A1

5.9

A1

5.9

A1

← 5.11

5.11d

5.10c

5.11d left crack

A1

alcove   flake

5.8

Happy Ledge bivy

5.8 Squeeze

A4

A3

A4

A1 crack right of corner

Florida Flake

s.b.

stance

A1   5.9

5.7

ledge

bivy

5.10b lb

s.b.

5.10-

5.9   flake

s.b.   5.10

slot   5.8

5.8

5.8

s.b.   5.8

4th Giants Staircase

5.10+

5.9

5.10

A1

5.10

5.9

5.10

5.10

← 5.7 —

Hardware

Via sin Liquor (A):
10 KBs
10 LAs
nuts
cams:
  3 ea. #0.5 to #2.5
  2 ea. #3 to #7
hooks
heads

Miscreant Wall (B):
4 LAs
2 ea. ½" to 1"
many nuts
Friends
hooks

Misty Wall (C):
nuts
cams:
  2 ea. #0.4 to #3
  1 ea. #3.5, #4
  1 - #4 Camalot

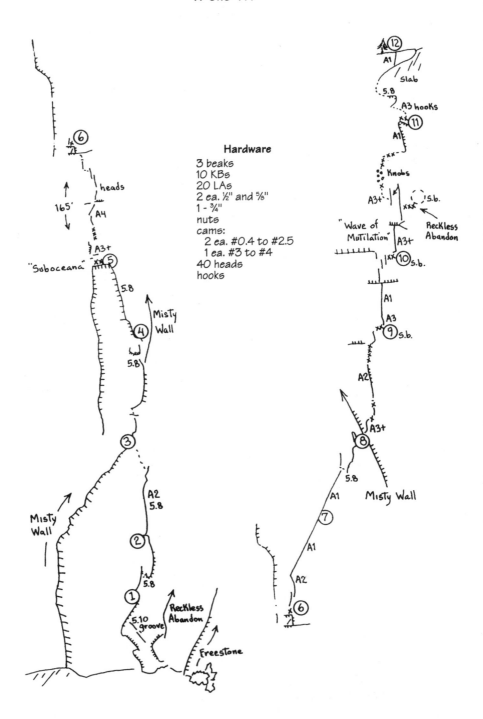

Hardware

3 beaks
10 KBs
20 LAs
2 ea. ½" and ⅝"
1 - ¾"
nuts
cams:
2 ea. #0.4 to #2.5
1 ea. #3 to #4
40 heads
hooks

Note: 24 holes.

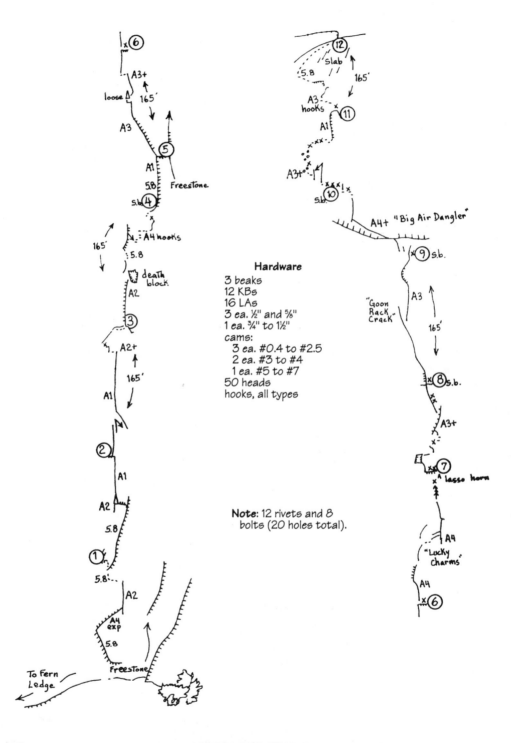

Hardware

3 beaks
12 KBs
16 LAs
3 ea. ½" and ⅝"
1 ea. ¾" to 1½"
cams:
  3 ea. #0.4 to #2.5
  2 ea. #3 to #4
  1 ea. #5 to #7
50 heads
hooks, all types

Note: 12 rivets and 8 bolts (20 holes total).

Aqua Vulva
(aka Route 66)
VI 5.10 A4

Photo on page 110.

Hardware

3 beaks
10 KBs
15 LAs
3 ea. ½" to ¾"
1 ea. 1" and 1¼"
nuts, including brass
cams:
  3 ea. #0.4 to #3
  2 - #4
  1 ea. #5 and #7
hooks, all types, including
  pointed Chouinards
40 heads
27 rivet hangers

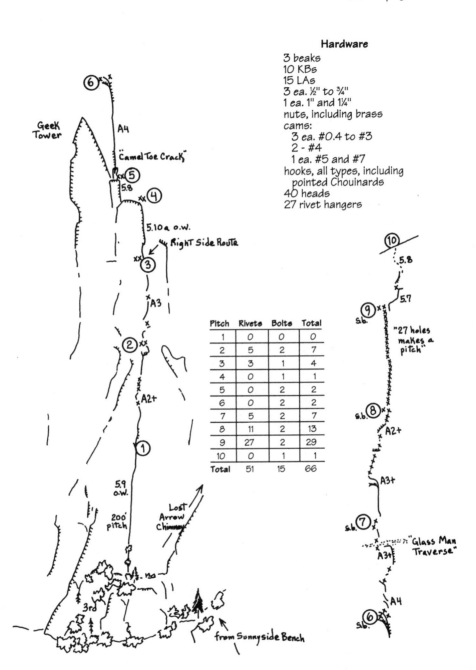

Pitch	Rivets	Bolts	Total
1	0	0	0
2	5	2	7
3	3	1	4
4	0	1	1
5	0	2	2
6	0	2	2
7	5	2	7
8	11	2	13
9	27	2	29
10	0	1	1
Total	51	15	66

Geek Tower

A4

"Camel Toe Crack"

5.8

5.10a o.w.

Right Side Route

A3

A2+

5.9 o.w.

200' pitch

Lost Arrow Chimney

3rd

from Sunnyside Bench

5.8

5.7

s.b.

"27 holes makes a pitch"

s.b. A2+

A3+

s.b.

"Glass Man Traverse"

A3+

A4

s.b.

Photo on page 110.

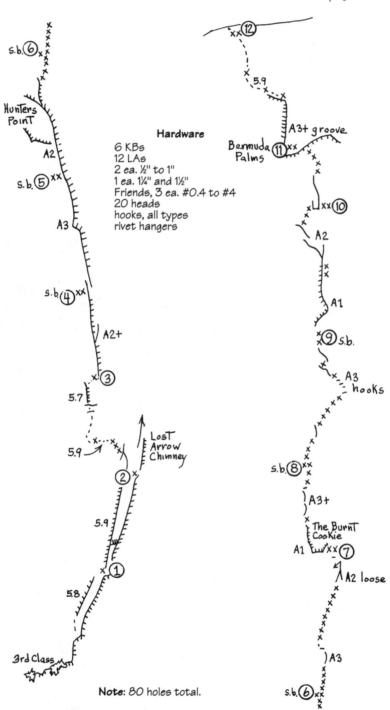

Hunters Point

A2

s.b. ⑤ ××

A3

s.b. ④ ××

A2+

③

5.7

5.9

Lost Arrow Chimney

②

5.9

⑤ s.b.

5.8

3rd Class

Hardware

6 KBs
12 LAs
2 ea. ½" to 1"
1 ea. 1¼" and 1½"
Friends, 3 ea. #0.4 to #4
20 heads
hooks, all types
rivet hangers

5.9

A3+ groove

Bermuda Palms ⑪ ××

⑩

A2

A1

⑨ s.b.

A3 hooks

s.b. ⑧ ××

A3+

The Burnt Cookie

A1 ⑦

A2 loose

A3

s.b. ⑥ ××

Note: 80 holes total.

Lost Arrow Spire
Direct Route
VI 5.11 A3
Lost Arrow Tip
5.12b or 5.8 A2

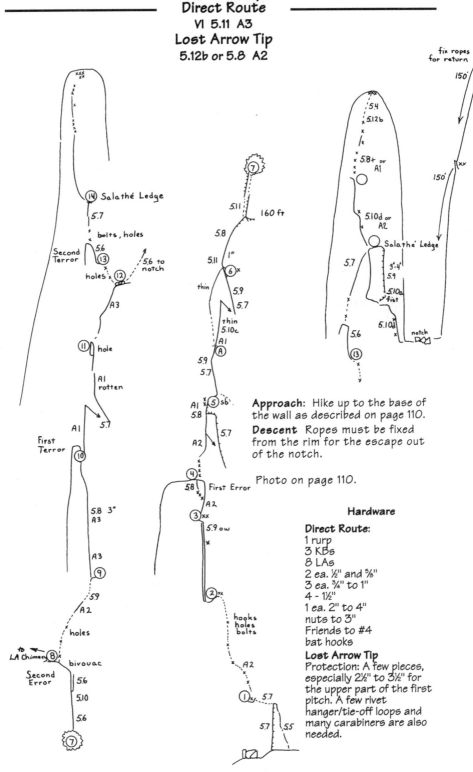

Salathé Ledge

5.7

bolts, holes

Second Terror

5.6

⑬

⑭

holes

⑫

5.6 to notch

A3

⑪ hole

A1 rotten

5.7

A1

First Terror

⑩

5.8 3"
A3

A3

⑨

5.9

A2

holes

to LA Chimney ⑧

bivouac

Second Error

5.6

5.10

5.6

⑦

5.11 160 ft

5.8

5.11 1"

⑥ x

thin

5.9

5.7

thin 5.10c

A1

Ⓐ

5.9
5.7

A1 x ⑤ sb

5.8

5.7

A2

④

5.8 First Error

A2

③ xx

5.9 ow

② xx

hooks
holes
bolts

A2

① x 5.7

5.7 .55

fix ropes for return

150'

5.4

5.12b

5.8+ or A1

150'

xx

5.10d or A2

Salathé Ledge

5.7

3"-4"
5.9

5.10a fist

5.10d

notch

5.6

⑬

Approach: Hike up to the base of the wall as described on page 110.

Descent Ropes must be fixed from the rim for the escape out of the notch.

Photo on page 110.

Hardware

Direct Route:
1 rurp
3 KBs
8 LAs
2 ea. ½" and ⅝"
3 ea. ¾" to 1"
4 - 1½"
1 ea. 2" to 4"
nuts to 3"
Friends to #4
bat hooks

Lost Arrow Tip
Protection: A few pieces, especially 2½" to 3½" for the upper part of the first pitch. A few rivet hanger/tie-off loops and many carabiners are also needed.

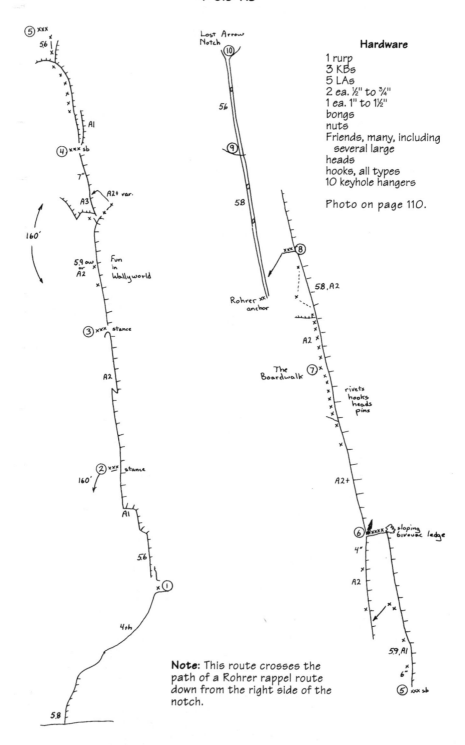

Hardware

1 rurp
3 KBs
5 LAs
2 ea. ½" to ¾"
1 ea. 1" to 1½"
bongs
nuts
Friends, many, including
  several large
heads
hooks, all types
10 keyhole hangers

Photo on page 110.

Note: This route crosses the path of a Rohrer rappel route down from the right side of the notch.

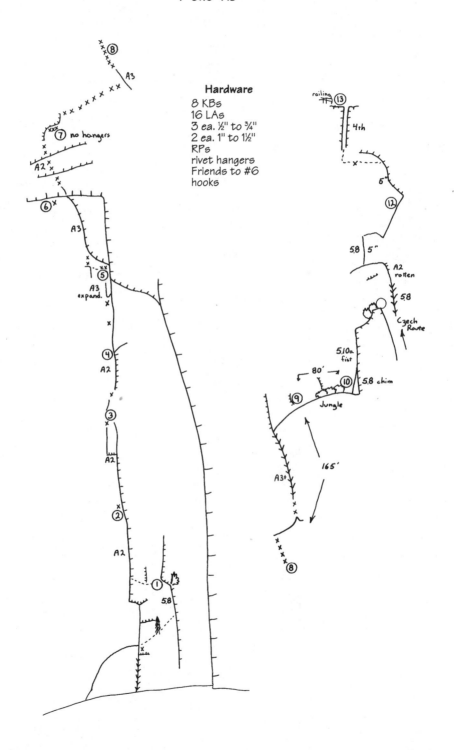

Hardware

8 KBs
16 LAs
3 ea. ½" to ¾"
2 ea. 1" to 1½"
RPs
rivet hangers
Friends to #6
hooks

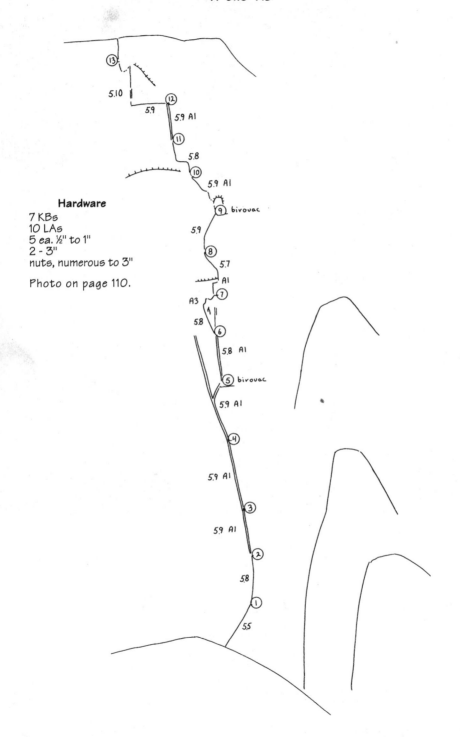

13

5.10

12

5.9

5.9 A1

11

5.8

10

5.9 A1

9 bivouac

Hardware
7 KBs
10 LAs
5 ea. ½" to 1"
2 - 3"
nuts, numerous to 3"

Photo on page 110.

5.9

8

5.7

A1

7

A3

5.8

6

5.8 A1

5 bivouac

5.9 A1

4

5.9 A1

3

5.9 A1

2

5.8

1

5.5

Royal Arches

1. Die Schweine von Oben
2. Toxic Waste Dump

Die Schweine von Oben
VI 5.11 A3+
Toxic Waste Dump
VI 5.8 A3+

Photo on page 123.

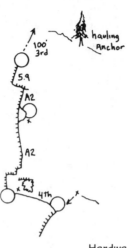

Hardware

Die Schweine von Oben (A):
10 KBs
15 LAs
3 ea. ½" to ¾"
2 ea. 1" and 1¼"
1 ea. 1½" to 3"
Friends to #4
hooks, all types
bolt hangers
keyhole hangers

Toxic Waste Dump (B):
Same as above, including:
  2 rurps
  30 heads, including circleheads

Approach: These climbs start at the high point of talus between Church Bowl and the Ahwahnee Hotel. Two approaches can be used. Either hike up from the Church Bowl at its far right side, or begin from the Ahwahnee Hotel. For the Ahwahnee option walk east a short distance along the horse trail. Follow the first creek bed up to the base of the wall, then to the top of the talus mound.

Descent: See page 125.

Bulging Puke
V 5.9 A4

Approach: From the Ahwahnee Hotel or North Pines Campground, take the trail toward Indian Caves. Before the caves are reached, however, head up north (near a point where the bike path and the horse trail almost touch), and follow the drainage that comes down from the left side of Washington Column. Meet the Column, then head left up steep talus. Continue left a short distance and negotiate slabs and ramps which trend up and right to the start of the route.

Descent: Routes that end atop Royal Arches or Washington Column necessitate a familiarity with North Dome Gully, the easiest access to and from the rim in the vicinity. The descent down North Dome Gully is the scene of frequent accidents. The trail from the top of the Column traverses east all the way to the forested gully and completely above the death slabs. Don't descend too early; if in doubt and contemplating rappels, keep traversing. If unfamiliar with the descent, don't attempt it at night.

Kelley Repp Ledge bivouac

A2

5.7

5.8

bolts
and
holes

Hardware

1 rurp
5 KBs
15 LAs
3 ea. ⅝" to 1¼"
2 ea. 1½" to 2"
1 ea. 2½" to 4"
heads
bat hooks

Photo on page 126.

5.10 or A2

A4

A2

O.W.

A2

Nada Ledge

A2

Gag Reflex Roof

A3

A3

poor belay

A4

Bile Duct Bypass

The Bile Duct

A3

A2

5.8

Washington Column:
South Face

1. Bulging Puke
2. South Central
3. Southern Man
4. South Face
5. Skull Queen

⑤

A1

A2

④ cave

5.10a
3-4"

x ⑬ expanding
5.8

A3

5.11 or A2
rotten

flakes

A2 or 5.10

5.9

② ⬊

2"
5.10c or A2
1"

x
①

5.9 o.w./squeeze
x

Dinner Ledge

±120 feet±

Hardware

1 rurp
2 KBs
5 LAs
3 ea. ½" to 1"
1 ea. 1¼" to 2"
Friends to #4, including one #7
hooks, small
nuts, including several ⅛" to ½"

Photo on page 126.

Approach: From the Ahwahnee Hotel or North Pines Campground, take the trail toward Indian Caves. Before the caves are reached however, head up north (near a point where the bike path and the horse trail almost touch), and follow the drainage that comes down from the left side of the column. A climber's trail skirts the base of the cliff all the way east to the bottom of North Dome Gully.

Descent: See page 125.

5.5

5.6

⑦

5.8

A1

⑥ good bivouac

A1

5.7 and tension   Top of the Mark

⑤

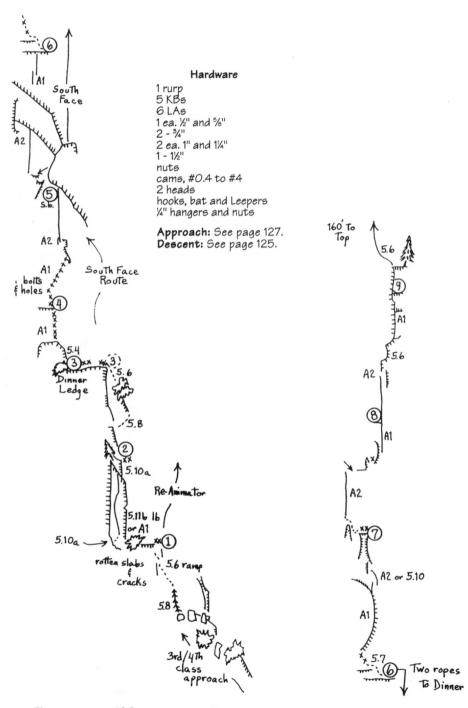

Hardware

1 rurp
5 KBs
6 LAs
1 ea. ½" and ⅝"
2 - ¾"
2 ea. 1" and 1¼"
1 - 1½"
nuts
cams, #0.4 to #4
2 heads
hooks, bat and Leepers
¼" hangers and nuts

Approach: See page 127.
Descent: See page 125.

South Face

A2

A1

South Face
Route

bolts
& holes

A1

5.4

Dinner
Ledge

5.6

5.8

5.10a

Re-Animator

5.11b 1b
or A1

5.10a

rotten slabs
& cracks

5.6 ramp

5.8

3rd/4th
class
approach

160' To
Top

5.6

A1

5.6

A2

A1

A2

A2 or 5.10

A1

5.7

Two ropes
To Dinner

Photo on page 126.

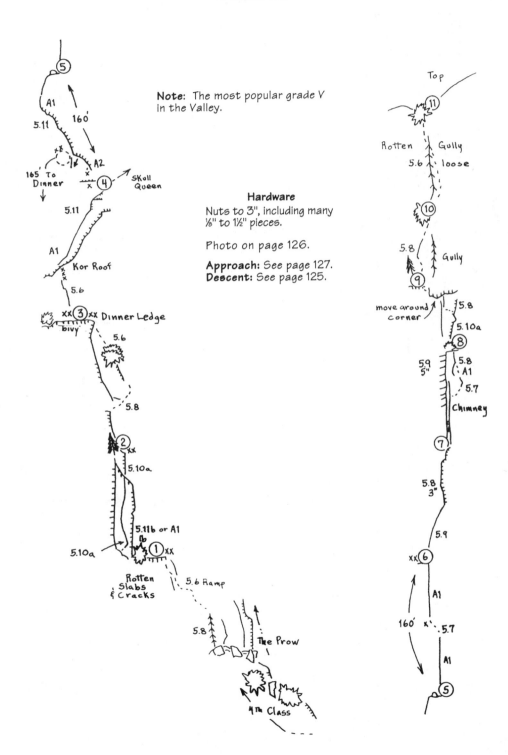

Note: The most popular grade V in the Valley.

Hardware

Nuts to 3", including many ⅛" to 1½" pieces.

Photo on page 126.

Approach: See page 127.
Descent: See page 125.

⑤

A1

5.11   160'

165' To Dinner   A2

5.11   Skull Queen

④

A1

Kor Roof

5.6

xx ③ xx Dinner Ledge
bivy

5.6

5.8

② xx

5.10a

5.11b or A1

5.10a   ① xx

Rotten Slabs & Cracks   5.6 Ramp

5.8   The Prow

4ᵗʰ Class

Top

⑪

Rotten   Gully

5.6   loose

⑩

5.8   Gully

⑨

move around corner   5.8

5.10a

⑧

5.9   5.8
5"   A1

5.7

Chimney

⑦

5.8
3"

5.9

xx ⑥

A1

160'   5.7

A1

⑤

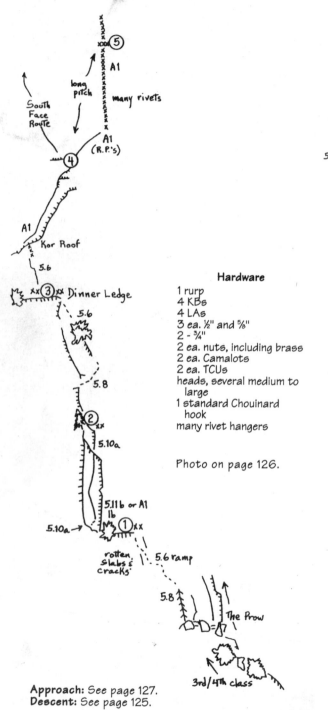

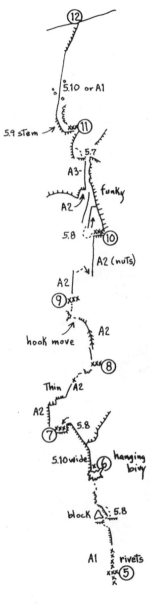

Hardware

1 rurp
4 KBs
4 LAs
3 ea. ½" and ⅝"
2 - ¾"
2 ea. nuts, including brass
2 ea. Camalots
2 ea. TCUs
heads, several medium to
  large
1 standard Chouinard
  hook
many rivet hangers

Photo on page 126.

Approach: See page 127.
Descent: See page 125.

Washington Column: East Face

6. The Re-animator
7. The Prow
8. Ten Days After
9. Electric Ladyland
10. Horney/Johnson

11. Mideast Crisis
12. Saddam Hussein
13. Great Slab Route
14. Bad Wall (V 5.8;A4)

The Re-animator
VI 5.8 A4

Approach: See page 127.
Descent: See page 125.

Photo on page 131.

Hardware

2 beaks
2 rurps
15 KBs
15 LAs
2 ea. ½" to ¾"
1 - 1"
wires
nuts, including ball nuts
  and wires
Friends:
  2 ea. #0.4 to #3
  1 ea. #3.5, #4, #5, #7
heads:
  3 - #1
  25 - #2
  15 - #3
  5 - #4
  5 - #5
hooks, all types, including
  pointed Chouinards
keyhole hangers

Note: 66 holes.

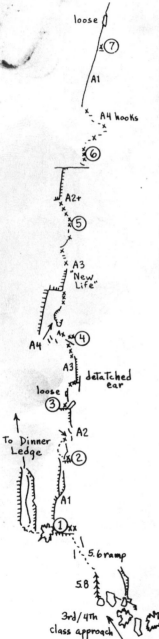

loose
(7)
A1
A4 hooks
(6)
A2+
(5)
A3 "New Life"
A4
(4)
A3
detatched ear
loose
(3)
A2
(2)
To Dinner Ledge
A1
(1) xx
5.6 ramp
5.8
3rd/4Th class approach

(11)
Thin 5.8
(10)
A3 KB's
edge of east & south faces
A2 hooks
(9)
hanging curtain of rock
A4
(8) xx
heads
"Give Em Enough Rope"
A3+
A4 hooks
loose
(7)

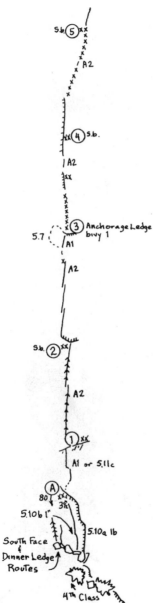

5.b ⑤ xx
x
x
x
A2 xxxxxx
x
x

xx ④ s.b.
┤ A2
xxx
xxxxxx
xxxx
x
x ③ Anchorage Ledge
5.7 ⸜ ⸝ bivy 1
┤ A1
x
┤ A2

s.b. ② xx

┤ A2

① xx
┤┤
A1 or 5.11c

Ⓐ
80 xxx
3½"
5.10b 1"
5.10a 1b
South Face
& Dinner Ledge
Routes
4th Class

⑪

Note: Steep
and exposed,
but straight-
forward.

⑩ x 3½"
belly crawl
5.9

A1
⑨

A2

⑧ Tapir Terrace
multi-level
bivy 1 or 2
x 5.7 ; A2
x
A2
x
⑦ x

The
Strange
Dihedral ┤ A2

x

xx ⑥ Stance
x
x

A2

⑤ xx
x
x

Hardware
Tiny nuts to 3½"
6 LAs
2 ea. ½" to 1½"
5 heads
hooks

Photo on page 131.

Approach: See page 127.
Descent: See page 125.

Photo on page 131.

Approach: See page 127.
Descent: See page 125.

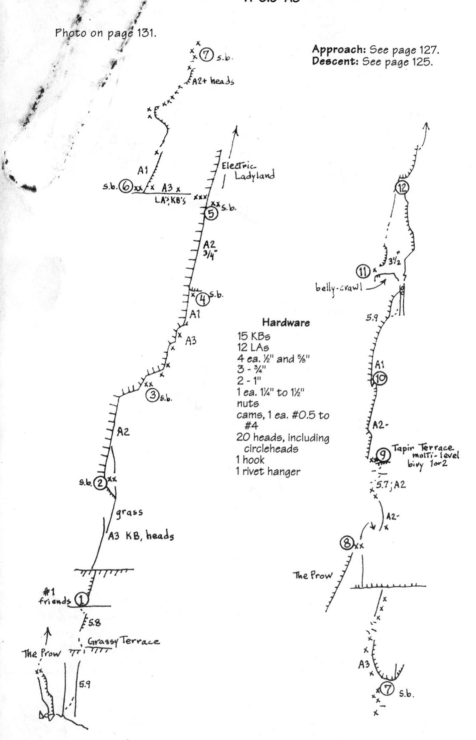

⑦ s.b.

A2+ heads

Electric
Ladyland

A1

s.b.⑥ xx x A3 x
LA's, KB's
xxx
xx s.b.
⑤

A2
3/4"

x ④ s.b.
A1

x A3

xx ③ s.b.

A2

s.b.②xx

grass

A3 KB, heads

#1
friends ①

5.8

The Prow Grassy Terrace

5.9

Hardware
15 KBs
12 LAs
4 ea. ½" and ⅝"
3 - ¾"
2 - 1"
1 ea. 1¼" to 1½"
nuts
cams, 1 ea. #0.5 to
  #4
20 heads, including
  circleheads
1 hook
1 rivet hanger

⑫

x 3½"

⑪ x
belly-crawl

5.9

A1
⑩

A2-

⑨ Tapir Terrace
xxx   multi-level
bivy 1 or 2

5.7; A2

A2-

⑧xx

The Prow

A3

⑦ s.b.

Approach: See page 127.
Descent: See page 125.

Photo on page 131.

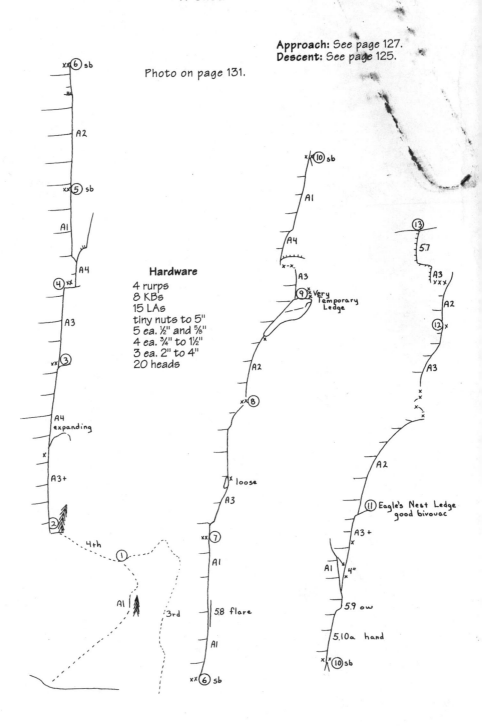

Hardware

4 rurps
8 KBs
15 LAs
tiny nuts to 5"
5 ea. ½" and ⅝"
4 ea. ¾" to 1½"
3 ea. 2" to 4"
20 heads

Approach: See page 127.
Descent: See page 125.

Photo on page 131.

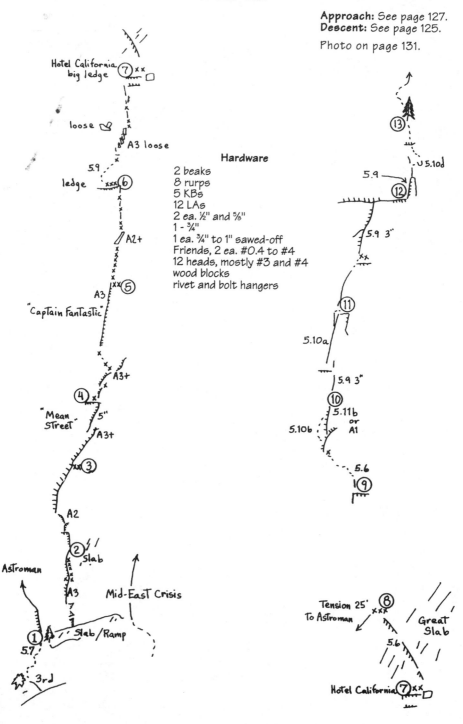

Hotel California
big ledge ⑦ xx

loose

A3 loose

5.9
ledge xxx ⑥

Hardware

2 beaks
8 rurps
5 KBs
12 LAs
2 ea. ½" and ⅝"
1 - ¾"
1 ea. ¾" to 1" sawed-off
Friends, 2 ea. #0.4 to #4
12 heads, mostly #3 and #4
wood blocks
rivet and bolt hangers

A2+

A3 xx ⑤
"Captain Fantastic"

A3+

④ x
"Mean
Street" 5"
A3+

xx ③

A2

② Slab

Astroman

A3

Mid-East Crisis

① A
5.7 Slab/Ramp

3rd

⑬

5.10d
5.9
⑫
5.9 3"
xx

⑪

5.10a
5.9 3"
⑩
5.11b
or
5.10b A1

5.6

⑨

Tension 25' ⑧
To Astroman xxx
Great
Slab
5.6
Hotel California ⑦ xx

Approach: See page 127.
Descent: See page 125.

Photo on page 131.

Hardware

7 KBs
15 LAs
4 ea. ½" to 1"
3 ea. 1¼" to 1½"
1 ea. 2" to 4"
Friends:
 3 ea. to #2.5
 2 ea. #3 to #4
2 hooks
nuts, many

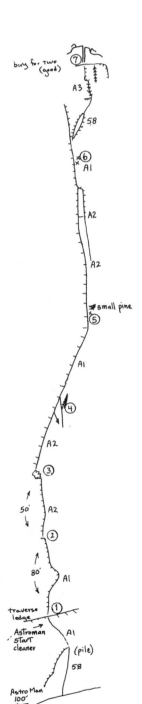

Saddam Hussein
V 5.9 A4

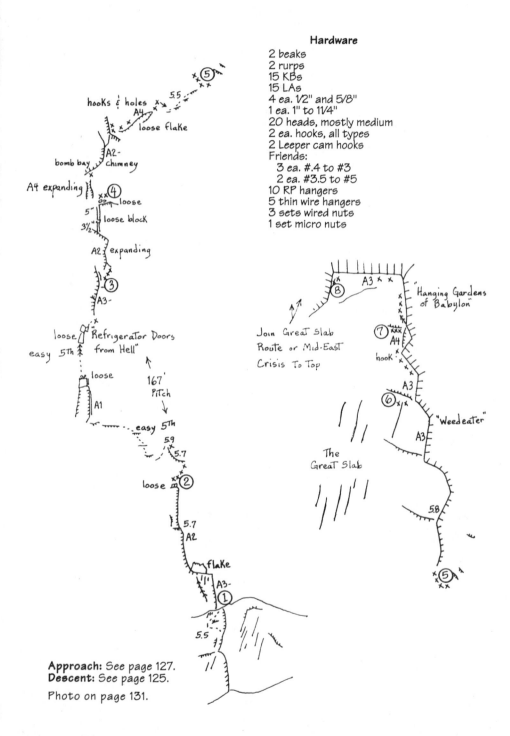

Hardware
2 beaks
2 rurps
15 KBs
15 LAs
4 ea. 1/2" and 5/8"
1 ea. 1" to 1 1/4"
20 heads, mostly medium
2 ea. hooks, all types
2 Leeper cam hooks
Friends:
  3 ea. #.4 to #3
  2 ea. #3.5 to #5
10 RP hangers
5 thin wire hangers
3 sets wired nuts
1 set micro nuts

hooks & holes
5.5
A4
loose flake
A2-
bomb bay chimney
A4 expanding
⑤
⑥
loose
5" loose block
3 1/2"
A2 expanding
③
A3-
loose
"Refrigerator Doors
easy 5th from Hell"
loose
167'
Pitch
A1
easy 5th
5.9
5.7
loose ②
5.7
A2
flake
A3-
①
5.5

⑧ A3
"Hanging Gardens
of Babylon"
Join Great Slab
Route or Mid-East
Crisis To Top
⑦
A4
hook
A3
⑥
"Weedeater"
A3
The
Great Slab
5.8
⑤

Approach: See page 127.
Descent: See page 125.

Photo on page 131.

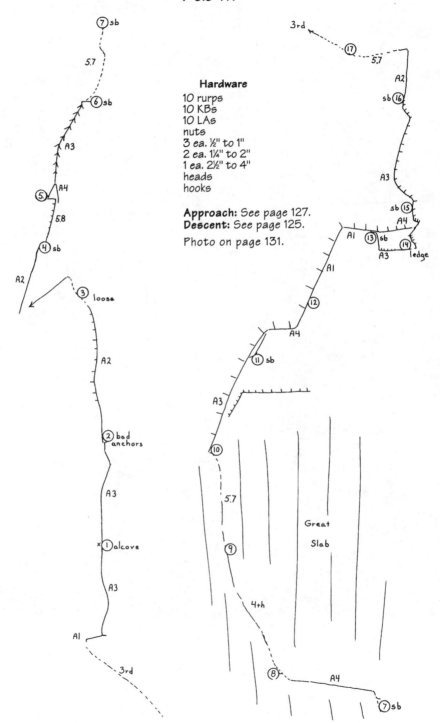

Hardware

10 rurps
10 KBs
10 LAs
nuts
3 ea. ½" to 1"
2 ea. 1¼" to 2"
1 ea. 2½" to 4"
heads
hooks

Approach: See page 127.
Descent: See page 125.

Photo on page 131.

Mt. Watkins: South Face

1. Hook, Line and Sinker
2. South Face Route
3. The Prism
4. Tenaya's Terror
5. Bob Locke Memorial Buttress
6. Escape From Freedom

Note: Major rock-fall suspected on this route.

Hardware

3 rurps
15 KBs
8 LAs
3 ea. ½" to 1½"
2 ea. 2" to 4"
many nuts to 6"
hooks, all types

Approach: Leave the Mirror Lake loop trail and follow a faint trail up the north side of Tenaya Canyon until beneath the scruffy right facing corner that lies under the center of the south face of Washington Column. Messy climbing, with some 5.9 leads to scree ledges.

Descent: Hike north and west off the top and pick up the Snow Creek Trail.

Photo on page 140.

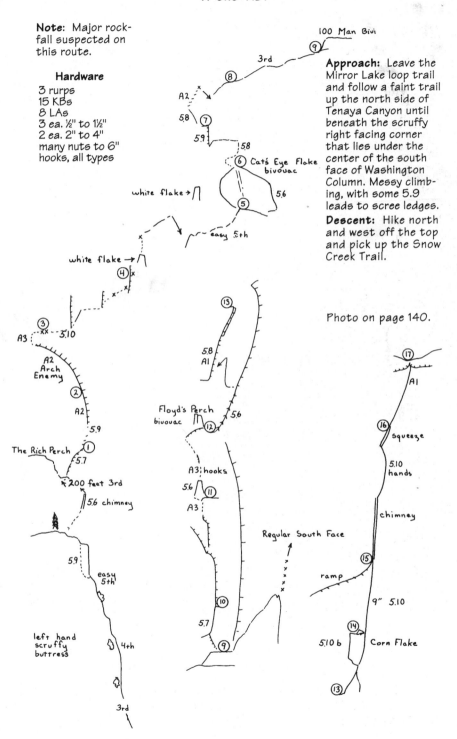

Photo on page 140.

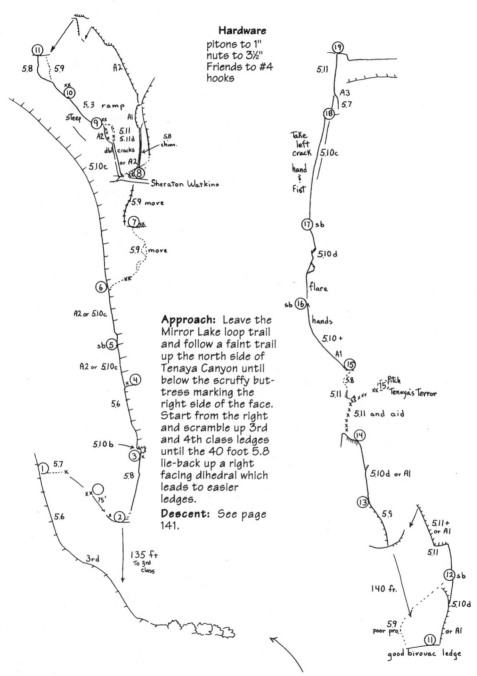

Hardware
pitons to 1"
nuts to 3½"
Friends to #4
hooks

5.8   5.9   A2

11

5.8   5.9   A2

xx
10

5.3 ramp

steep

9   xx
A2   f   5.11
dbl   5.11d
cracks
or A2
5.10c
A1   5.8 chim.

xx
8   Sheraton Watkins

5.9 move

7   xx

5.9 move

xx
6

A2 or 5.10c

sb 5

A2 or 5.10c

4   xx

5.6

5.10b

3   xx

1   5.7   x

xx   75'

5.6

5.8

2

3rd

135 ft
To 3rd class

19   5.11

A3
18   5.7

Take
left
crack   5.10c

hand
&
Fist

17   sb

5.10d

flare

sb 16

hands

5.10+

A1
15

5.8   15 Pitch
5.11   xx xx Tenaya's Terror

x 5.11 and aid

14

5.10d or A1

13   5.9

5.11+
or A1

5.11

12 sb

140 ft.

5.10d

5.9
poor pro.

11   or A1

good bivouac ledge

Approach: Leave the Mirror Lake loop trail and follow a faint trail up the north side of Tenaya Canyon until below the scruffy buttress marking the right side of the face. Start from the right and scramble up 3rd and 4th class ledges until the 40 foot 5.8 lie-back up a right facing dihedral which leads to easier ledges.

Descent: See page 141.

Tenaya's Terror
VI 5.9 A4

Photo on page 140.

Approach: Scramble up to the start of the route as for the **South Face** route.

Descent: See page 141.

Hardware
2 rurps
10 KBs
20 LAs
3 ea. ⅝" to 1"
2 ea. 1¼" to 1½"
Friends:
  2 ea. to #4
  1 - #6
10 heads
hooks
rivet hangers

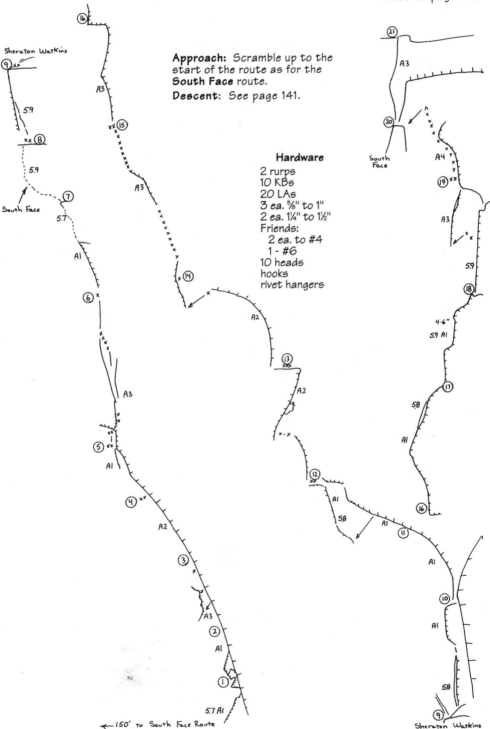

Photo on page 140.

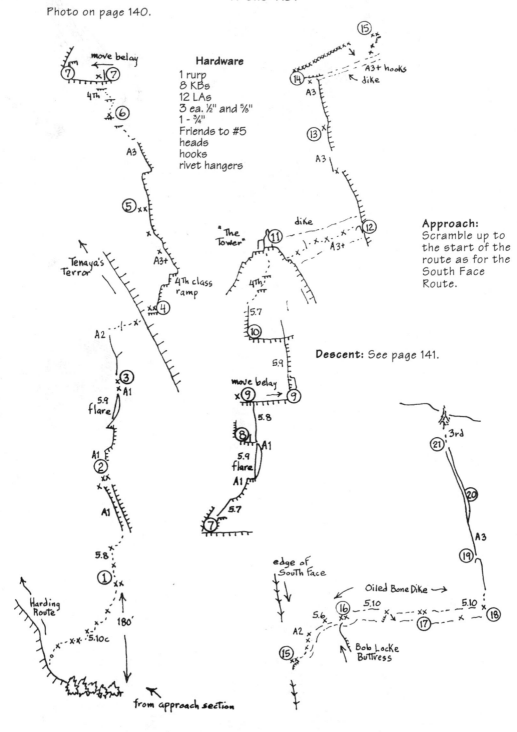

Hardware

1 rurp
8 KBs
12 LAs
3 ea. ½" and ⅝"
1 - ¾"
Friends to #5
heads
hooks
rivet hangers

Approach:
Scramble up to
the start of the
route as for the
South Face
Route.

Descent: See page 141.

Approach: Scramble up to the start of the route as for the South Face Route.

Descent: See page 141.

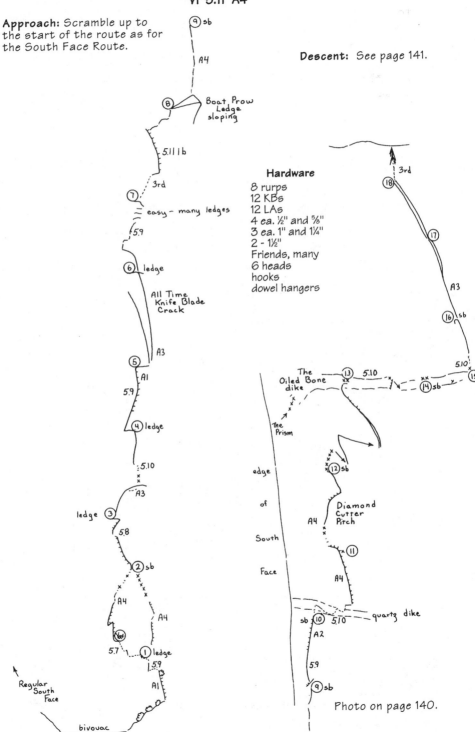

Hardware

8 rurps
12 KBs
12 LAs
4 ea. ½" and ⅝"
3 ea. 1" and 1¼"
2 - 1½"
Friends, many
6 heads
hooks
dowel hangers

Photo on page 140.

Escape from Freedom
V/VI 5.11c A1

Photo on page 140.

Descent: See page 141.

Note: 1 pendulum, 2 tension traverses, 2 points of aid.

Protection
Tiny to #3.5 Friends

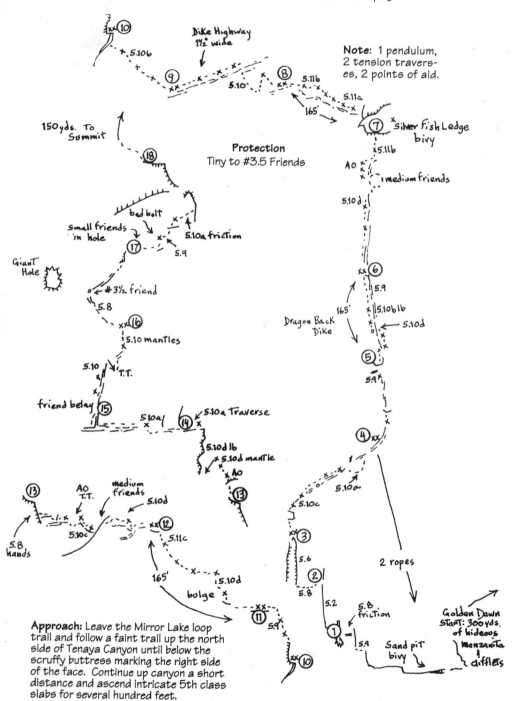

Approach: Leave the Mirror Lake loop trail and follow a faint trail up the north side of Tenaya Canyon until below the scruffy buttress marking the right side of the face. Continue up canyon a short distance and ascend intricate 5th class slabs for several hundred feet.

rockfall
area

3

1

2

Photo courtesy of US Department of the Interior, National Park Service, Yosemite National Park

Quarter Dome

1. East Quarter Dome, North Face
2. East Quarter Dome, Route of All Evil
3. West Quarter Dome, North Face

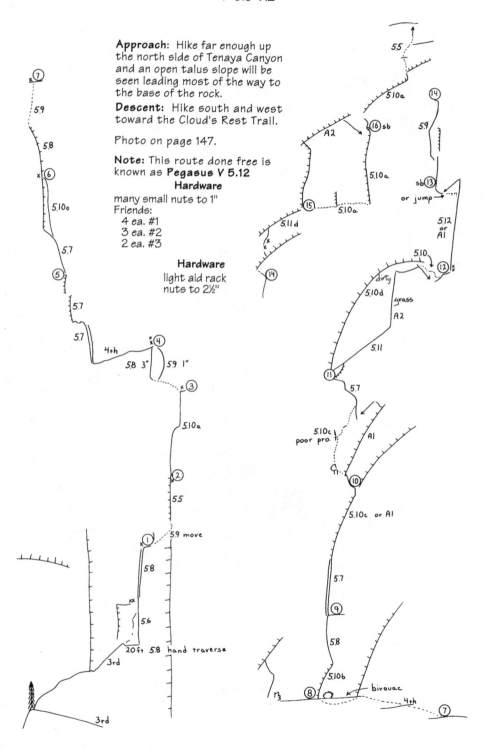

Approach: Hike far enough up the north side of Tenaya Canyon and an open talus slope will be seen leading most of the way to the base of the rock.

Descent: Hike south and west toward the Cloud's Rest Trail.

Photo on page 147.

Note: This route done free is known as **Pegasus V 5.12**
Hardware
many small nuts to 1"
Friends:
4 ea. #1
3 ea. #2
2 ea. #3

Hardware
light aid rack
nuts to 2½"

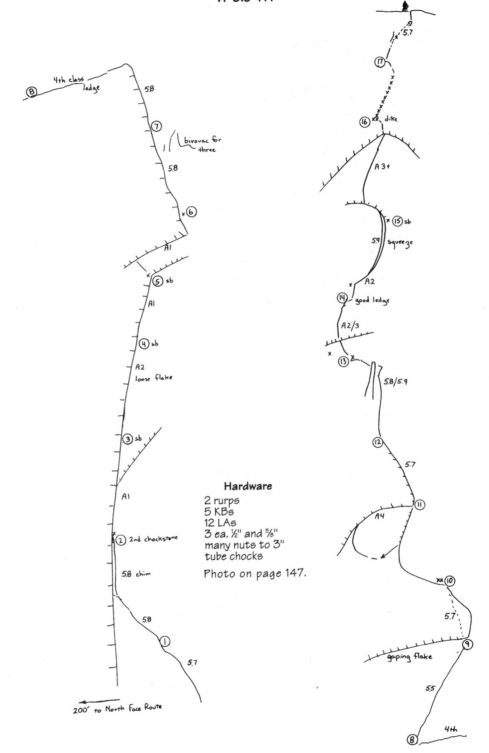

⑧ — 4th class ledge

5.8

⑦

bivouac for three

5.8

⑥

A1

⑤ sb

A1

④ sb

A2 loose flake

③ sb

A1

② 2nd chockstone

5.8 chim

5.8

①

5.7

200' to North Face Route

5.7

⑰

⑯ dike

A3+

⑮ sb

5.9 squeeze

A2

⑭ good ledge

A2/3

⑬

5.8/5.9

⑫

5.7

⑪

A4

xx ⑩

5.7

⑨

gaping flake

5.5

⑧ 4th

Hardware

2 rurps
5 KBs
12 LAs
3 ea. ½" and ⅝"
many nuts to 3"
tube chocks

Photo on page 147.

Hardware
2 rurps
5 KBs
10 LAs
many nuts to 2"

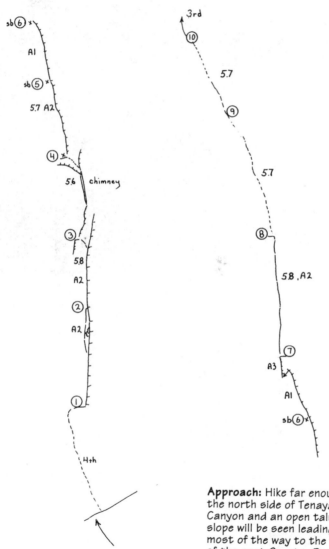

3rd

10

5.7

9

5.7

8

5.8 , A2

7

A3

A1

sb 6 ✗

sb 6 ✗

A1

sb 5 ✗

5.7 A2

4 ✗

5.6 chimney

3

5.8

A2

2

A2

1

4th

Approach: Hike far enough up the north side of Tenaya Canyon and an open talus slope will be seen leading most of the way to the base of the east Quarter Dome. Work west through brush to the base of the rock.

Photo on page 147.

Half Dome: Northwest Face

1. Northwest Buttress
2. Regular Northwest Face
3. Arcturas
4. Direct Northwest Face
5. Queen of Spades

6. Tis-sa-ack
7. The Kali Yuga
8. Zenith
9. Bushido

Approach: For all Half Dome Northwest Face routes, hike up the trail from Happy Isles to the eastern shoulder of Half Dome (about 7.5 miles). From the broad wooded ridge before the cables and sandy switchbacks, drop down and around to the base of the northwest face via a climber's trail. A quicker, more direct, yet very devious approach can be made from the vicinity of Mirror Lake. In general, this begins somewhat upstream from Mirror Lake, trending up and right, with the final section ascending beneath **Tis-sa-ack.**

Descent: From the summit, pick up cables that lead to the trail down.

Approach and Descent: See page 151.

Photo on page 151.

Hardware

3 rurps
3 KBs
12 LAs
4 ea. ½" to 1½"
1 ea. 2" to 3"

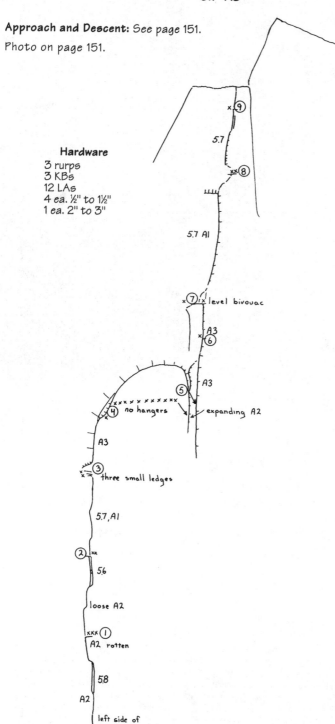

5.7

x ⑨

xx ⑧

5.7 AI

x ⑦ x level bivouac

x A3
⑥

A3

⑤

④ no hangers → ← expanding A2

A3

③ three small ledges

5.7, AI

② xx

5.6

loose A2

xxx ①

A2 rotten

5.8

A2

left side of
main arch

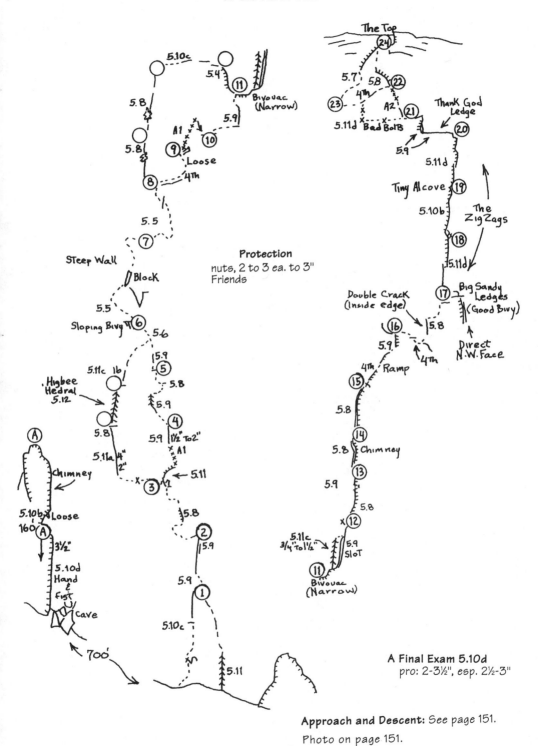

The Top
24

5.7   5.8   22
4th
23   A2   21   Thank God
5.11d Bad Bolts   20   Ledge
5.9
5.11d
Tiny Alcove   19
5.10b   The
ZigZags
18
5.11d

Double Crack   17   Big Sandy
(Inside edge)   5.8   Ledges
(Good Bivy)
16
5.9   Direct
4th   N.W. Face
4th   Ramp
15
5.8
14
5.8 Chimney
13
5.9
5.8
5.11c   X   12
3/4" To1 1/2"   5.9
Slot
11
Bivouac
(Narrow)

5.10c   5.4
11
5.8   Bivouac
A1   (Narrow)
5.9
9   10
5.8   Loose
8   4th

5.5
7

Steep Wall
Block

5.5
Sloping Bivy   6   5.6
5.9
5.11c 1b   5
5.8
Higbee   5.9
Hedral   4
5.12   5.9 1 1/2" To 2"
5.8   A1
A   5.11a 4"
2"
Chimney   X   3
5.11
5.10b Loose
160 A   5.8
3 1/2"
5.10d   2
Hand   5.9
& Fist
Cave   5.9
1
700'   5.10c
5.11

Protection
nuts, 2 to 3 ea. to 3"
Friends

A Final Exam 5.10d
pro: 2-3 1/2", esp. 2 1/2-3"

Approach and Descent: See page 151.

Photo on page 151.

Hardware
4 rurps
4 KBs
12 LAs
4 ea. ½" to 1½"
3 - 2"
1 ea. 2½" to 4"

Approach and Descent:
See page 151.

Photo on page 151.

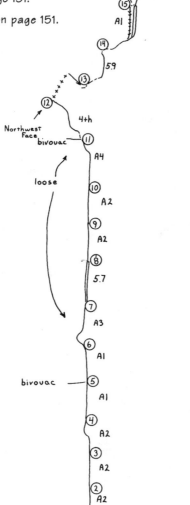

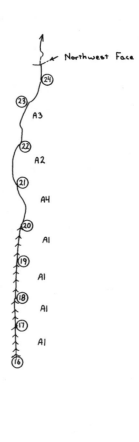

Northwest Face

16

15

Al

Northwest Face

14

5.9

13

12

4+h

Northwest
Face
bivouac

11

A4

loose

10

A2

9

A2

8

5.7

7

A3

6

Al

bivouac

5

Al

4

A2

3

A2

2

A2

1

Northwest
Face
Route

A2
5.7

60 ft

Northwest Face

24

23

A3

22

A2

21

A4

20

Al

19

Al

18

Al

17

Al

16

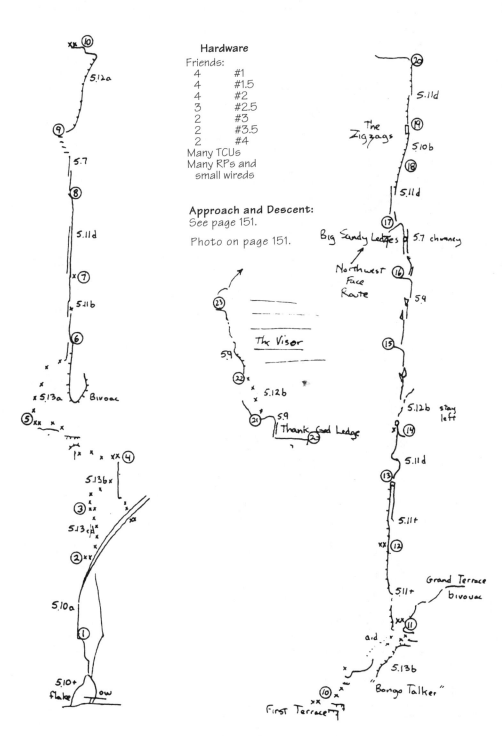

Hardware

Friends:

4	#1
4	#1.5
4	#2
3	#2.5
2	#3
2	#3.5
2	#4

Many TCUs
Many RPs and
small wireds

Approach and Descent:
See page 151.

Photo on page 151.

Photo on page 151.

Approach and Descent:
See page 151.

Hardware

10 rurps
25 KBs
15 LAs
5 ea. ½" to ¾"
1 - 1"
nuts, including ball nuts
tubes to 8"
Friends, 4 sets including #5s
hooks
keyhole hangers

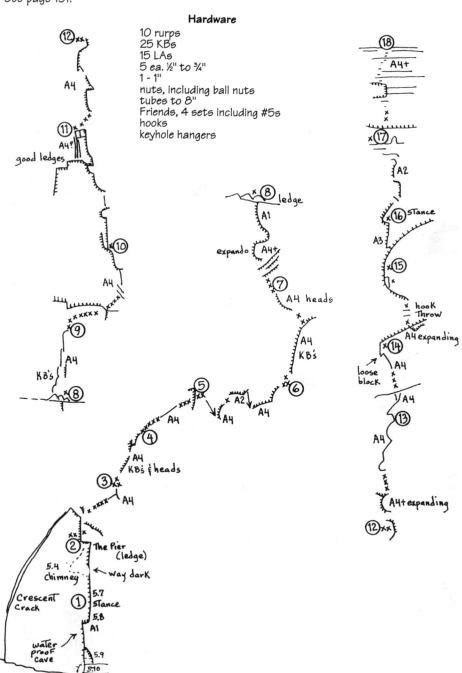

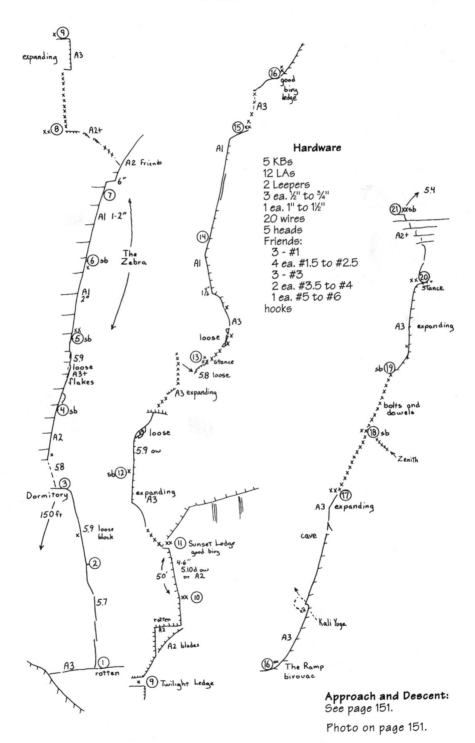

Hardware

5 KBs
12 LAs
2 Leepers
3 ea. ½" to ¾"
1 ea. 1" to 1½"
20 wires
5 heads
Friends:
  3 - #1
  4 ea. #1.5 to #2.5
  3 - #3
  2 ea. #3.5 to #4
  1 ea. #5 to #6
hooks

Approach and Descent:
See page 151.

Photo on page 151.

Hardware

5 beaks
3 rurps
20 KBs
5 bugaboos, long
18 LAs
3 ea. ½" and ⅝"
2 - ¾"
1 ea. 1" to 1½"
cams, 2½ sets ea.
   #0.4 to #4
1 set ball nuts
35 heads
hooks, including
   large and pointed
   Chouinards
20 slings
10 RP (keyhole)
   hangers
2 alternating 165'
   lead ropes recom-
   mended

Approach and Descent:
See page 151.

Photo on page 151.

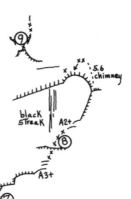

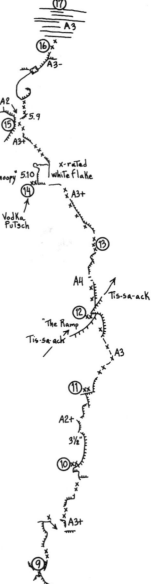

Pitch	Rivets	Bolts	Total
1	0	0	0
2	0	0	0
3	0	0	0
4	11	2	13
5	5	1	6
6	16	2	18
7	9	1	10
8	3	3	6
9	2	2	4
10	9	2	10
11	0	1	1
12	10	2	12
13	8	3	11
14	12	2	14
15	14	1	15
16	4	2	6
17	0	0	0
Totals	103	24	127

All rivets ⅚" machine bolt
   (¾" to 1")
Belay bolts are ⅚" button
   head or ⅜" machine bolts.

Photo on page 151.

Hardware

8 rurps
20 KBs
20 LAs (mostly long)
6 - ½"
5 - ⅝"
2 - ¾"
3 sets of cams to #3
  Camalot, include one
  each #4 and #5
  Camalot

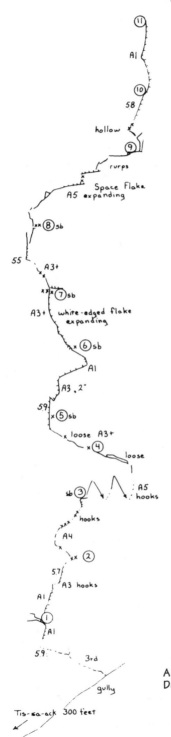

Approach and
Descent: See page 151.

The White Room

VI 5.10 A4

Hardware

#3 to #6 beaks
8 rurps, including a few ground down
20 KBs, including long thin bugaboos
20 LAs
4 ea. ½" and ⅝"
3 - ¾"
1 - 1"
1 Leeper

cams:
 2 ea. #0.4 and #0.5
 3 ea. #.75 to #3
 2 ea. #3.5 to #4
heads (52 total):
 #1 - 3 regular, 2 circle
 #2 - 25 regular, 4 circle
 #3 - 10 regular, 3 circle
 #4 - 5 regular, 0 circle
hooks, all types, including regular and large claw
6 keyhole hangers

Approach and Descent: See page 151.

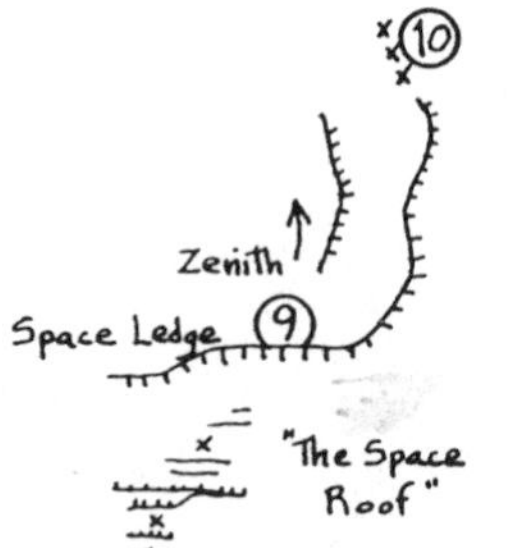

10
Zenith
Space Ledge
9
"The Space Roof"

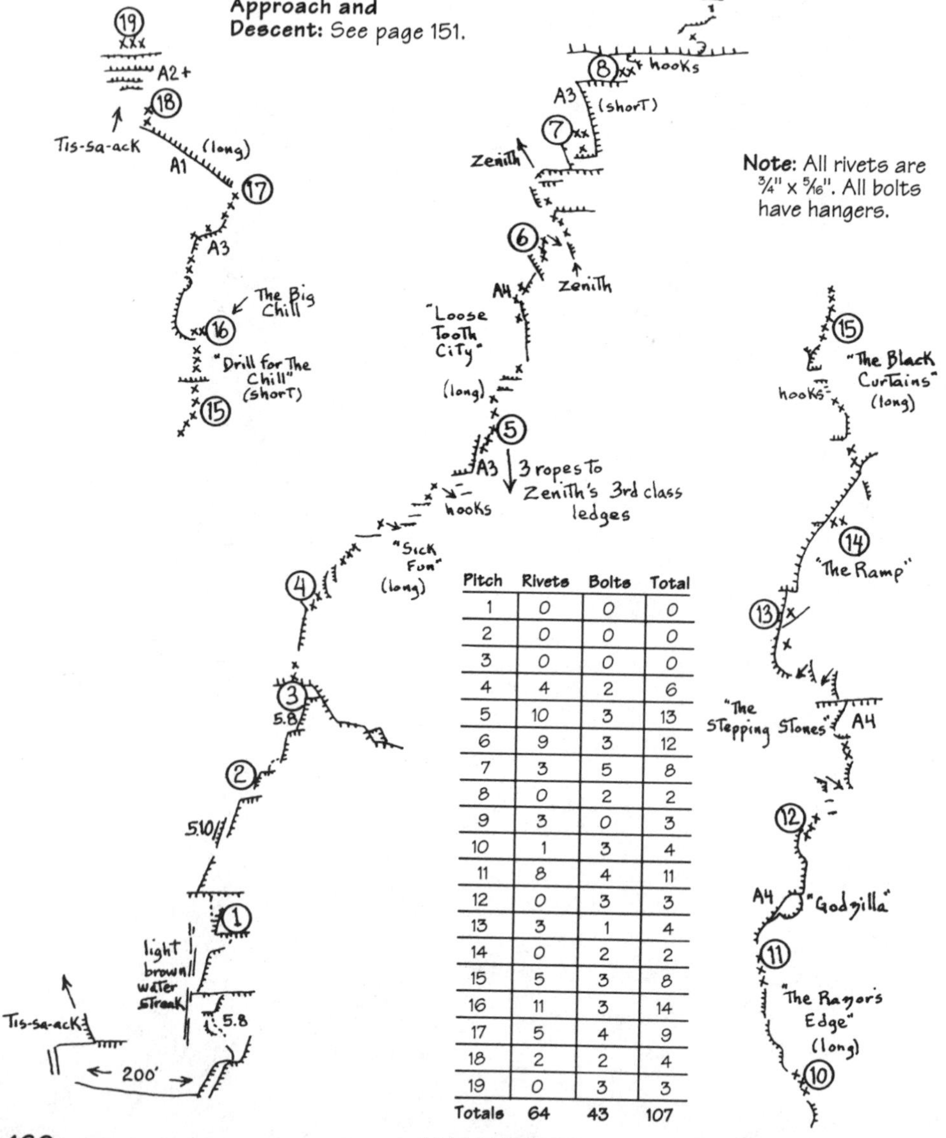

19
A2+
18
Tis-sa-ack
(long)
A1
17
A3
The Big Chill
16
"Drill for The Chill"
(shorT)
15
8
hooks
A3
(shorT)
7
Zenith
6
Zenith
A4
"Loose Tooth City"
(long)
5
A3
3 ropes To Zenith's 3rd class ledges
hooks
"Sick Fun"
(long)
4
3
5.8
2
5.10
1
light brown water streak
5.8
Tis-sa-ack
200'
15
"The Black Curtains"
(long)
hooks
14
"The Ramp"
13
"The Stepping Stones"
A4
12
A4
"Godzilla"
11
"The Razor's Edge"
(long)
10

Note: All rivets are ¾" x 5⁄16". All bolts have hangers.

Pitch	Rivets	Bolts	Total
1	0	0	0
2	0	0	0
3	0	0	0
4	4	2	6
5	10	3	13
6	9	3	12
7	3	5	8
8	0	2	2
9	3	0	3
10	1	3	4
11	8	4	11
12	0	3	3
13	3	1	4
14	0	2	2
15	5	3	8
16	11	3	14
17	5	4	9
18	2	2	4
19	0	3	3
Totals	64	43	107

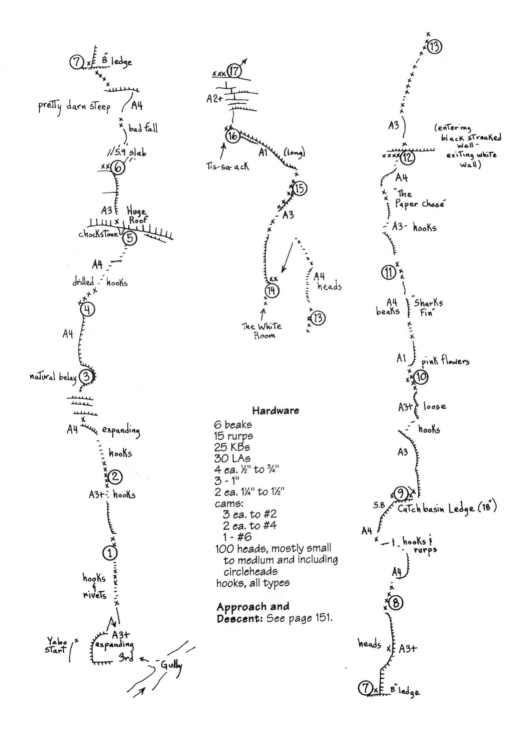

⑦ x 8" ledge

pretty darn steep   A4

bad fall

// 5.9 slab

xx ⑥

A3 Huge Roof

chockstone ⑤

A4

drilled - hooks

xxx ④

A4

natural belay ③

A4 expanding

hooks

xxx ②

A3+ : hooks

xx ①

hooks & rivets

Yabo Start

A3+ expanding 3rd

Gully

xxx ⑰

A2+

⑯   A1 (long)

Tis-sa-ack

⑮

A3

xx ⑭

A4 heads

The White Room

⑬

Hardware

6 beaks
15 rurps
25 KBs
30 LAs
4 ea. ½" to ¾"
3 - 1"
2 ea. 1¼" to 1½"
cams:
 3 ea. to #2
 2 ea. to #4
 1 - #6
100 heads, mostly small
 to medium and including
 circleheads
hooks, all types

**Approach and
Descent:** See page 151.

⑬

A3   (entering black streaked wall - exiting white wall)

xxxx ⑫

A4   "The Paper chase"

- A3- hooks

⑪ x

A4 beaks   "Sharks Fin"

A1 } pink flowers

x ⑩

A3+ } loose

- hooks

A3

⑨

5.8   Catch basin Ledge (18")

A4

x -¦- hooks & rurps

A4

x ⑧

heads x | A3+

⑦ x 8" ledge

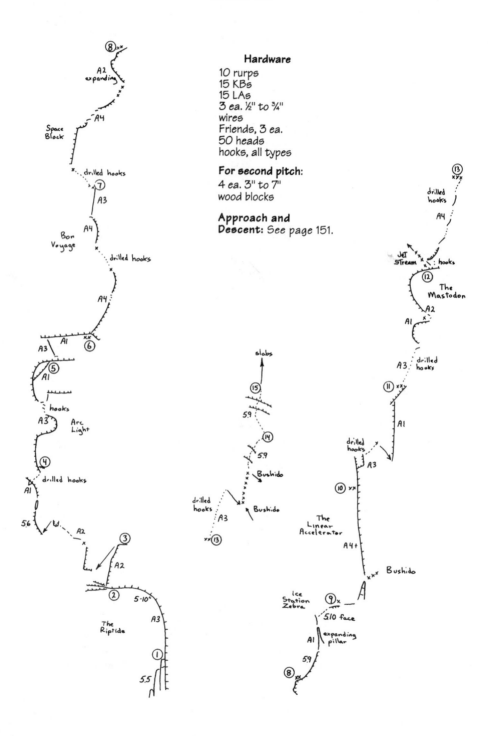

Hardware

10 rurps
15 KBs
15 LAs
3 ea. ½" to ¾"
wires
Friends, 3 ea.
50 heads
hooks, all types

For second pitch:
4 ea. 3" to 7"
wood blocks

**Approach and
Descent:** See page 151.

Bushido
VI 5.9 A4

Approach and Descent: See page 151.

Photo on page 151.

Hardware

3 rurps
14 KBs
14 LAs
3 ea. ½" to 1"
1 ea. 1¼" to 1½"
nuts
cams:
  4 ea. to #4
  1 ea. #6 and #8
hooks
keyhole hangers

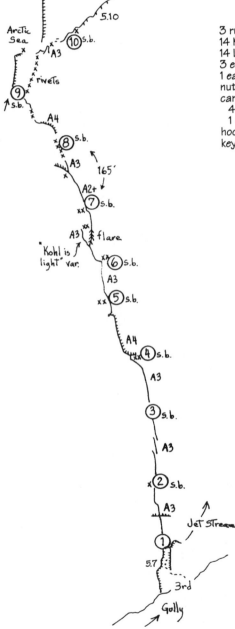
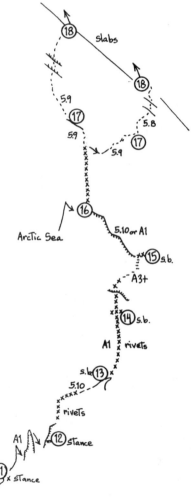

HALF DOME ————————

**Approach and
Descent:** See page 151.

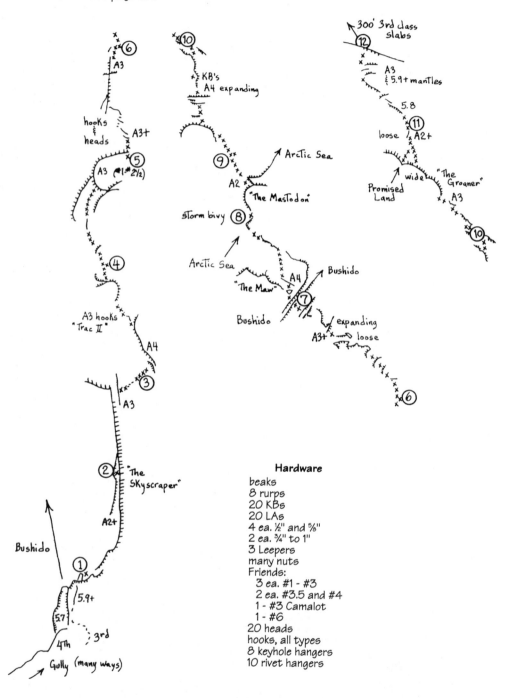

Hardware

beaks
8 rurps
20 KBs
20 LAs
4 ea. ½" and ⅝"
2 ea. ¾" to 1"
3 Leepers
many nuts
Friends:
  3 ea. #1 - #3
  2 ea. #3.5 and #4
  1 - #3 Camalot
  1 - #6
20 heads
hooks, all types
8 keyhole hangers
10 rivet hangers

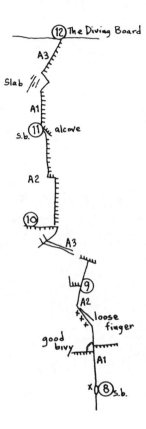

Note: As of publication date, this route is closed to climbing from January 1 to August 1 to protect peregrine falcon nesting sites. Check with the National Park Service for updated information.

Approach: This route climbs the steep, white wall below The Diving Board; a crest of rock forming the shoulder immediately right of the Northwest Face of Half Dome. Starting somewhat upstream from Mirror Lake, trend up and right as per the approach for Half Dome, yet several hundred feet before reaching **Tis-sa-ack** contour out right on a ledge pattern to attain the start of the route.

Descent Head straight back along the Southwest Face of Half Dome. Follow a climber's trail (the Snake Dike approach in reverse) through brush and over slabs which angle toward the South Face. Then when feasible drop down into brush trails to reach Lost Lake, the marsh at the eastern foot of Mt. Broderick. From here continue to hike over the broad eastern flank of Liberty Cap to merge with the horse/foot trail about ⅓ mile above Nevada Fall.

(12) The Diving Board

A3

Slab

A1

s.b. (11) alcove

A2

(10)

A3

(9)

A2

loose finger

good bivy

A1

x (8) s.b.

A1

s.b. x (8) "The Red Line"
A1

A3

x
A4

"Gunning for The Red Line"
(bad fall)

(7) xx bivy

A2

"handle with care"

loose roof

(6)

5.7
no pro.

(5)

5.10b

(4)

5.9

fix down (3)
2 ropes

5.10a

5.10a

Note: Right of approach slabs to Half Dome.

5.8 (2)

(1)

5.9

Hardware
20 KBs
20 LAs
3 ea. ½" and ⅝"
2 - ¾"
1 - 1"
wires
Friends:
 3 sets #1 to #3
 1 - #4

Half Dome: South Face

1. Lost Again
2. South Face Route
3. Southern Belle
4. Karma

Approach: Use Happy Isles trail.
Descent: From the summit, pick up cables that lead to the trail down.

Photo on page 166.

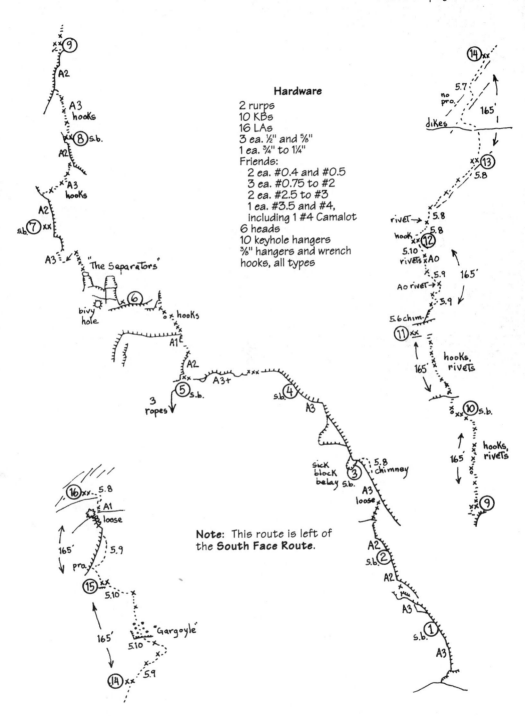

Hardware

2 rurps
10 KBs
16 LAs
3 ea. ½" and ⅝"
1 ea. ¾" to 1¼"
Friends:
   2 ea. #0.4 and #0.5
   3 ea. #0.75 to #2
   2 ea. #2.5 to #3
   1 ea. #3.5 and #4,
    including 1 #4 Camalot
6 heads
10 keyhole hangers
⅜" hangers and wrench
hooks, all types

Note: This route is left of
the **South Face Route.**

Hardware

3 KBs
18 LAs, mostly short
3 ea. ½" to ¾"
2 ea. 1"
1 ea. 1¼" to 1½"
Friends:
  1 ea. #½-#¾
  2 ea. #1 to #3½
  1 ea. #4, #5, #6
wired nuts, many for use as rivet
  hangers
1 ea. Chouinard hook
bat hooks
self-locking ⅜" keyhole hangers

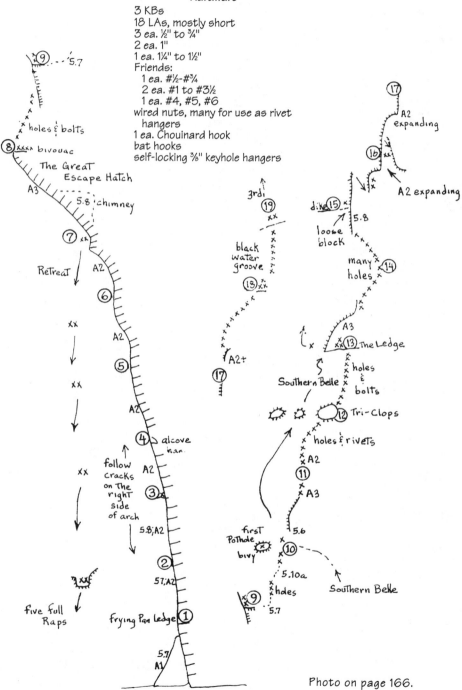

Photo on page 166.

Karma
V 5.11d A0

Approach: Hike up to this part of the south face from the trail to the top of Half Dome, cutting left when the wall becomes close.

Hardware

Friends, 1 ea. to #4,
    including 1/2 and 3/4
nuts
slings
bolt kit
bat hooks
2 ropes recommended

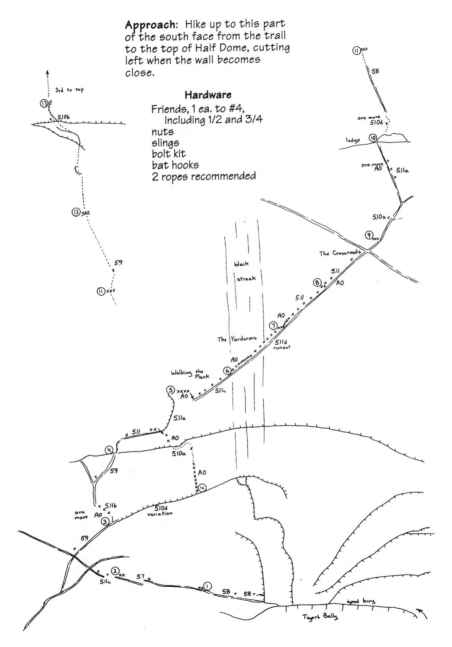

3rd to top

⑬

5.10b

⑫

5.9

⑪

⑪

5.8

one more
5.10d

ledge ⑩

one more
A0   5.11a

5.10a

⑨

The Crossroads

black streak

5.11

⑧   A0

5.11

A0

⑦

The Yardarms

5.11d
runout

A0

Walking the Plank

⑥

5.11c

⑤   A0

5.11a

5.11   A0

④   5.10a

5.9

A0

⑦

one move   5.11b
A0

③   5.10d variation

5.9

②   5.7

5.11c

①   5B   5B

apod bivy

Tiger's Belly

Photo on page 166.

Photo on page 166.

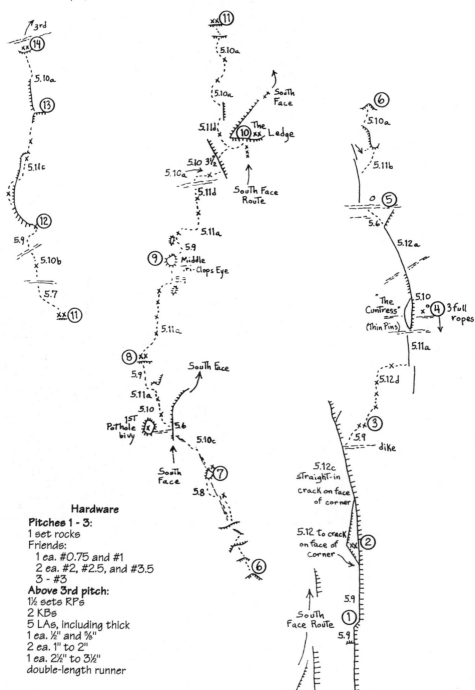

Hardware

Pitches 1 - 3:
1 set rocks
Friends:
  1 ea. #0.75 and #1
  2 ea. #2, #2.5, and #3.5
  3 - #3

Above 3rd pitch:
1½ sets RPs
2 KBs
5 LAs, including thick
1 ea. ½" and ⅝"
2 ea. 1" to 2"
1 ea. 2½" to 3½"
double-length runner

Liberty Cap

1. West Buttress
2. Southwest Face
3. Direct Southwest Face

Approach: Hike up to all the Liberty Cap routes from Happy Isles.

West Buttress
V 5.10 A3

Photo on page 171.

Hardware

15 KBs
15 LAs
3 ea. ½" and ⅝"
5 ea. ¾" to 1"
3 ea. 1¼" to 1½"
2 - 2"
1 ea. 2½" to 3"
Friends, 2 ea. to #4

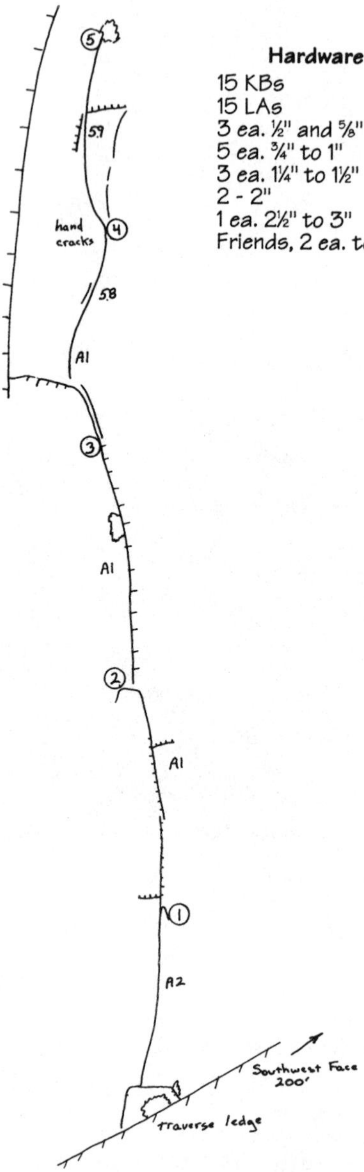

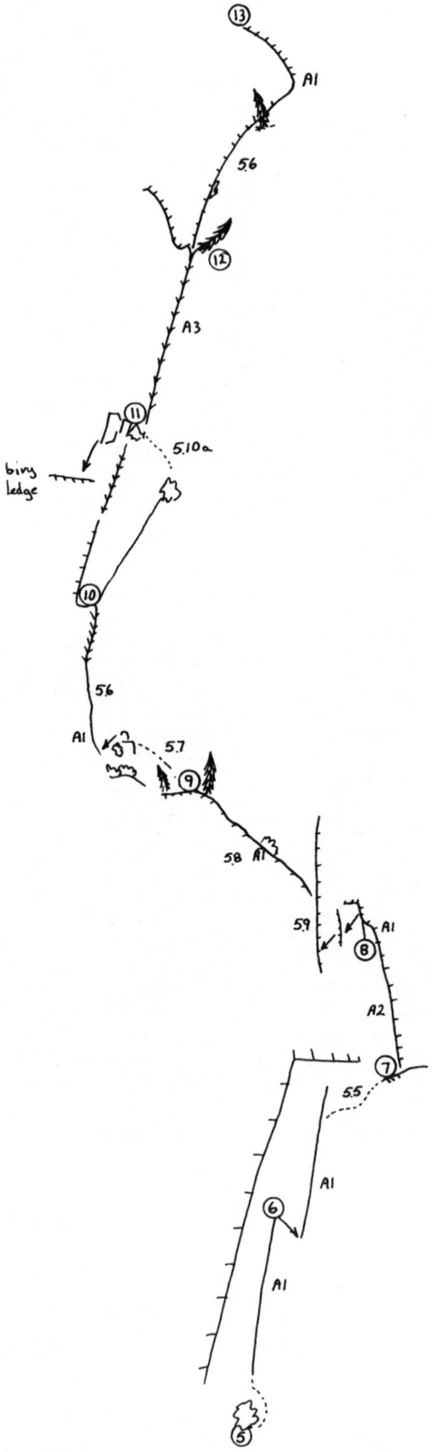

Photo on page 171.

Hardware

5 KBs
12 LAs
3 ea. ½" to 1½"
2 ea. 2" to 3"
nuts to 3½"
Friends, 2 ea. to #4
hooks

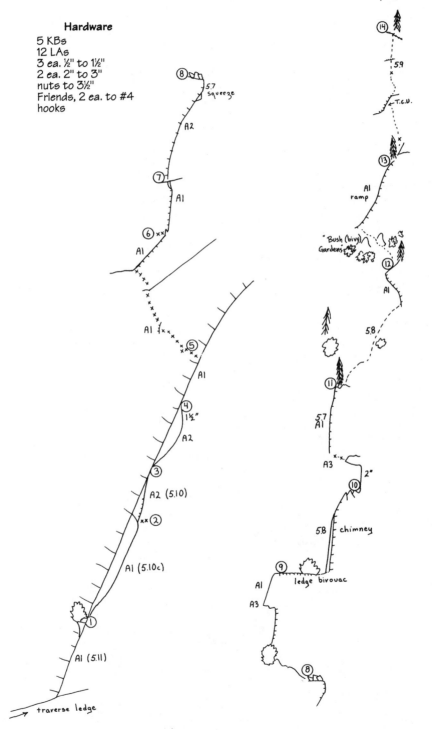

⑧ 5.7 squeeze

A2

⑦ A1

⑥ ×× A1

A1 ×× ⑤

A1

④ 1½"

A2

③

A2 (5.10)

×× ②

A1 (5.10c)

① A1 (5.11)

traverse ledge

⑭

5.9 ×

T.C.U.

× ⑬

A1 ramp

"Bush (bivy) Gardens" ⑫

A1

5.8

⑪

5.7 A1

A3 ×–×

⑩ 2"

5.8 chimney

⑨ ledge bivouac

A1

A3

⑧

Photo on page 171.

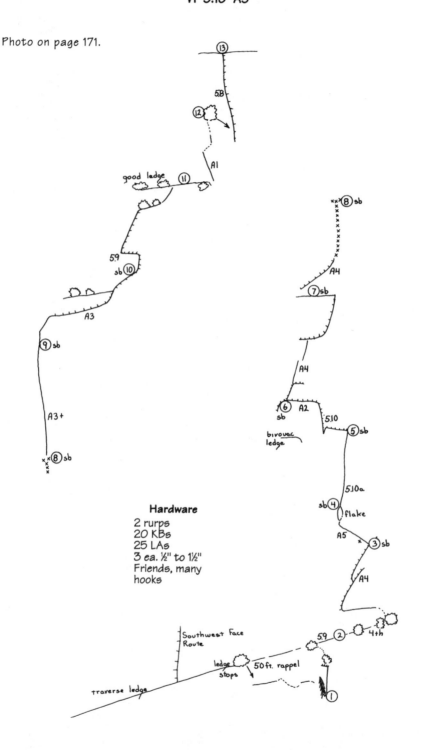

Hardware

2 rurps
20 KBs
25 LAs
3 ea. ½" to 1½"
Friends, many
hooks

Note: This route is located on the south side of the rock.

Hardware

5 rurps
6 KBs
6 LAs
4 ea. ½" and ⅝"
3 ea. ¾" to 1½"
nuts to 3½"
heads, small
hooks

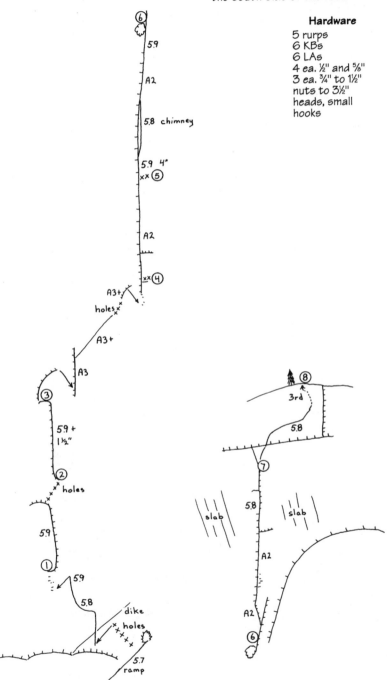

Bananarama
V 5.10a A3

Approach:
Panorama Cliff is the dark grey wall between Vernal and Illilouette Falls. This route ascends the left margin of a blank, shield-like area on the formation. The horse trail from Happy Isles forms a useful portion of the approach.

Descent: Continue up the slope to gain the Panorama/Nevada Falls Trail for return to Yosemite Valley.

⑪ Bungi
A2

⑩

⑨ A3
4"-6"

⑧

A3
4"-6"

⑦

A3

Banana Rama Ledge ⑥

5.7;A2

⑤

2nd class

horn ④

5.7;A1

Hardware
5 KBs
15 LAs
1 ea. bong
4 ea. ½", ⅝", ¾" and 1"
3 ea. 1¼", 1½"
RPs
stoppers
Friends, numerous
hooks
1 rivet hanger

③

4th class

② 2nd class

① 5.0

⑰
A1

⑯
A2

ledge

⑮

⑭ 4th;A1

5.10a

⑬
A1

⑫

A1

Bungi
(good ledge
⑪

Ice Age
VI 5.8 A5

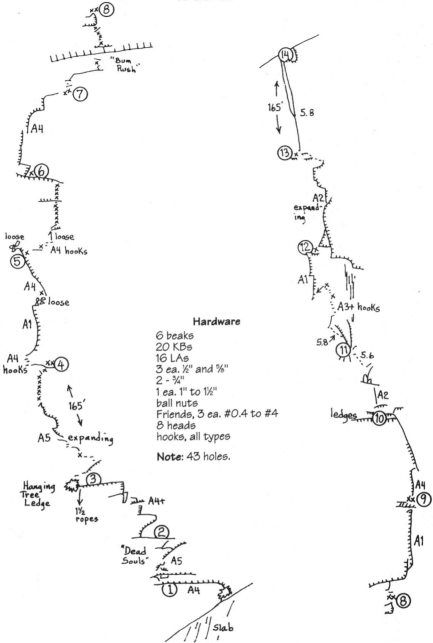

Hardware

6 beaks
20 KBs
16 LAs
3 ea. ½" and ⅝"
2 - ¾"
1 ea. 1" to 1½"
ball nuts
Friends, 3 ea. #0.4 to #4
8 heads
hooks, all types

Note: 43 holes.

Approach: This route ascends the large white recess on the major wall below and somewhat north of Glacier Point. Follow the old Ledge Trail that begins right of the Glacier Point Apron, behind Curry Village.

Descent: The gully on the right side of the formation is followed down to the LeConte Memorial — or in summer months one may continue hiking the Ledge Trail (class 2) to Glacier Point.

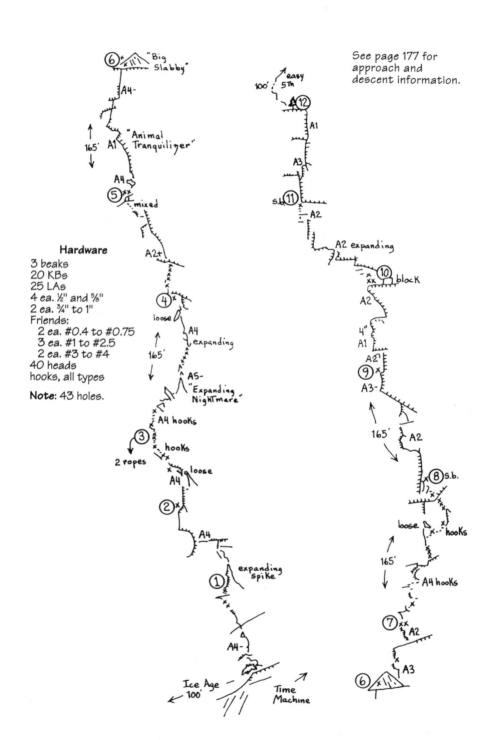

See page 177 for approach and descent information.

"Big Slabby"

A4-

"Animal Tranquilizer"

165' A1

A4

⑤ mixed

Hardware

3 beaks
20 KBs
25 LAs
4 ea. ½" and ⅝"
2 ea. ¾" to 1"
Friends:
  2 ea. #0.4 to #0.75
  3 ea. #1 to #2.5
  2 ea. #3 to #4
40 heads
hooks, all types

Note: 43 holes.

A2+

④

loose

A4 expanding

165'

A5-
"Expanding Nightmare"

A4 hooks

③ hooks

2 ropes

loose

A4

②

A4

expanding spike

①

A4-

Ice Age
← 100'

Time Machine

easy 5th
100'

⑫ A1

A3

s.b. ⑪

A2

A2 expanding

⑩ block

A2

4"
A1

A2

⑨ A3-

165' A2

⑧ s.b.

loose hooks

165'

A4 hooks

⑦ A2

⑥ A3

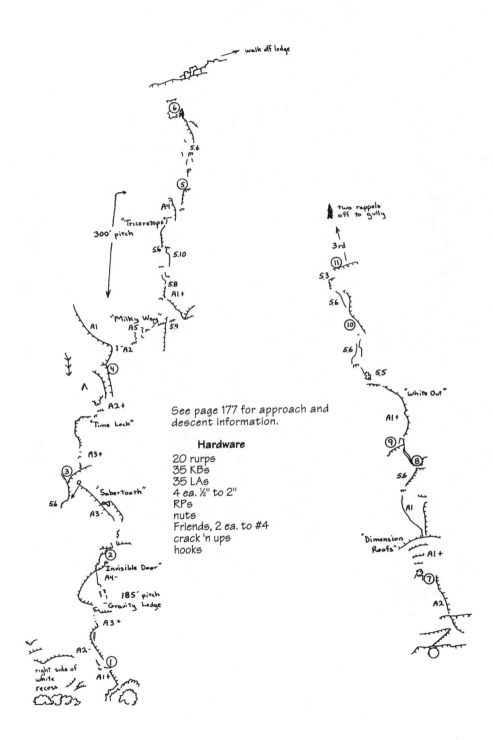

walk off ledge

two rappels off to gully

3rd

5.6

5.3

5.6

5.6

5.5

"White Out"

A1+

5.6

A1

"Dimension Roofs"

A1+

A2

5.6

5.6

A4

"Triceratops"

300' pitch

5.6 5.10

5.8
A1+

"Milky Way"
A5 ?
A2

5.9

A1

A2+

"Time Lock"

A3+

"Sabertooth"

5.6

A3-

See page 177 for approach and descent information.

Hardware
20 rurps
35 KBs
35 LAs
4 ea. ½" to 2"
RPs
nuts
Friends, 2 ea. to #4
crack 'n ups
hooks

"Invisible Door"
A4-

185' pitch
"Gravity Ledge"

A3+

A2-

right side of white recess

A1+

Sentinel Rock: North Face

1. Flashback
2. Direct North Face

3. Gobi Wall
4. Flying Buttress Direct

Hardware

3 rurps
20 KBs
15 LAs
3 - ½"
4 ea. to 1¼"
3 - 1½"
2 - 2"
1 - 2½"
stoppers
Friends:
 2 ea. #1 to #1.5
 3 ea. #2 - #3
 2 - #3.5
 2 - #4
3 heads
hooks
rivet hangers

Photo on page 180.

Approach: The routes on the north and west faces of Sentinel Rock are approached by 3rd class ledges that traverse up and right across the lower broken area of the formation. First, hike up the Four-Mile Trail for about a mile to the stream that comes down from the east side of the rock. Leave the trail and hike up the streambed several hundred feet and move over to the prominent ramp that starts the long scramble up and right. This leads to the base of the Flying Buttress, an 800-foot pillar that sits at the right side of the flat north face and is the start of the **Flying Buttress Direct**. The routes on the west face are around the corner. The routes on the north face require further scrambling up and left on ledges. Allow two hours approach time from Camp Four.

Descent: From the summit, work south to the notch behind Sentinel Rock via manzanita tunnels that skirt small outcrops. From the notch, scramble down the loose, Class 2 gully that leads east to a stream. Further down, descend improbable terrain in the middle of a scruffy buttress that separates two chasms. Eventually the Four-Mile Trail is reached.

Direct North Face
V 5.12a

Approach and Descent: See page 181.
First Free Ascent: Kevin Thaw, Adam
Wainwright, Oct. '94.

Photo on page 180.

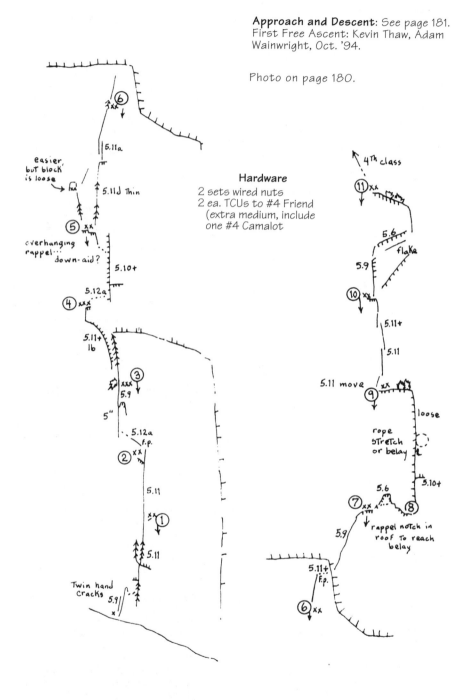

easier,
but block
is loose

5.11a

5.11d Thin

⑤ xx

overhanging
rappel...
down-aid?

5.10+

5.12a

④ xxx

5.11+
lb

⑥ xx

③
5.9

5"

5.12a
f.p.

② xx

5.11

①

5.11

Twin hand
cracks 5.9
x

Hardware
2 sets wired nuts
2 ea. TCUs to #4 Friend
(extra medium, include
one #4 Camalot

4th class

⑪ xx

5.6
flake

5.9

⑩ xx

5.11+

5.11

5.11 move   xx
⑨

loose

rope
stretch
or belay

5.10+

5.6
⑦ xx
⑧
rappel notch in
roof to reach
belay

5.9

5.11+
f.p.

⑥ xx

Approach and Descent: See page 181.

Photo on page 180.

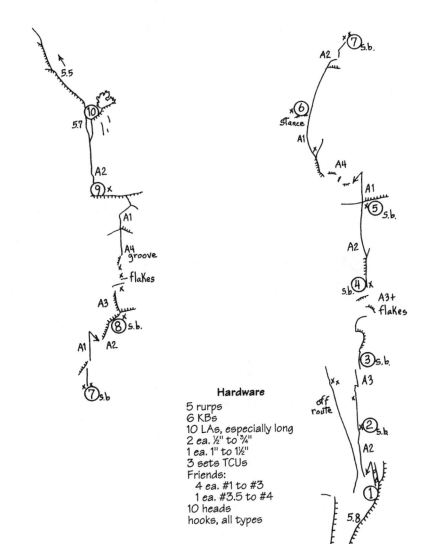

Hardware

5 rurps
6 KBs
10 LAs, especially long
2 ea. ½" to ¾"
1 ea. 1" to 1½"
3 sets TCUs
Friends:
  4 ea. #1 to #3
  1 ea. #3.5 to #4
10 heads
hooks, all types

Approach and Descent: See page 181.

Photo on page 180.

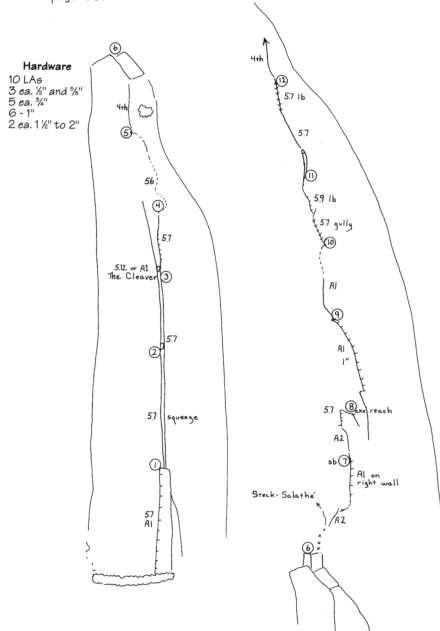

Hardware

10 LAs
3 ea. ½" and ⅝"
5 ea. ¾"
6 - 1"
2 ea. 1 ½" to 2"

In Cold Blood
V 5.11b A3

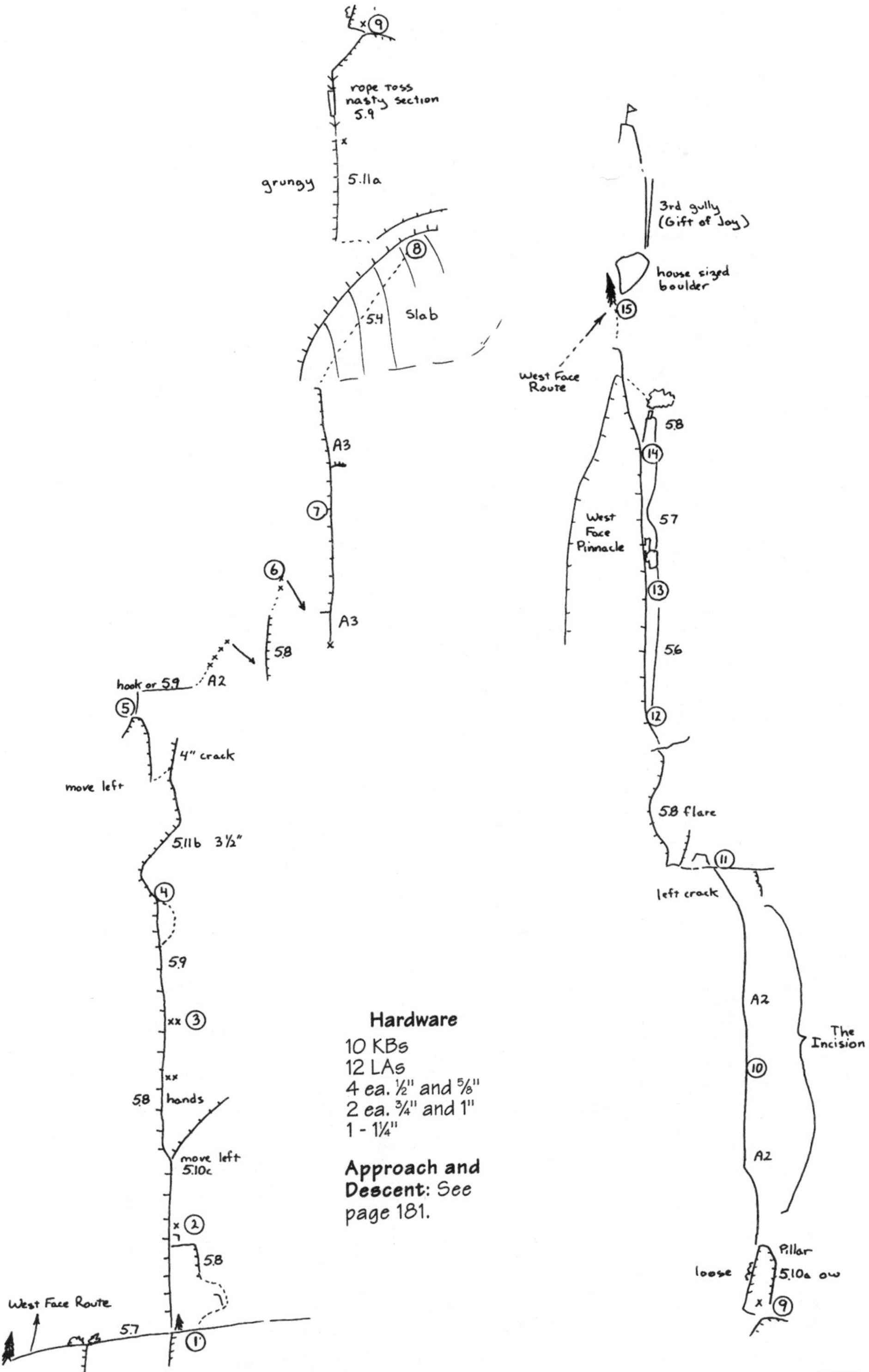
rope toss
nasty section
5.9
grungy
5.11a
5.4
Slab
A3
A3
5.8
hook or 5.9
A2
4" crack
move left
5.11b 3½"
5.9
5.8
hands
move left
5.10c
5.8
West Face Route
5.7
3rd gully
(Gift of Joy)
house sized
boulder
West Face
Route
5.8
West
Face
Pinnacle
5.7
5.6
5.8 flare
left crack
A2
The
Incision
A2
Pillar
loose
5.10a ow

Hardware
10 KBs
12 LAs
4 ea. ½" and ⅝"
2 ea. ¾" and 1"
1 - 1¼"

Approach and Descent: See page 181.

Approach: The routes of Higher Cathedral Spire and Higher Cathedral Rock is made from the climbers' trail up the Spires Gully. Start hiking at a road turnout 1.4 miles east of the Hwy 41/Hwy 140 junction at Bridalveil Falls. The trails heads directly back and up into the woods.

Hardware

2 KBs
6 LAs
3 ea. ½" and ⅝"
6 ea. ¾" to 1"
4 ea. 1½" to 2"
2 ea. 2½" to 3"

Descent: Rappel the **Regular Route** (not described in this book) that follows the southwest corner of the spire.

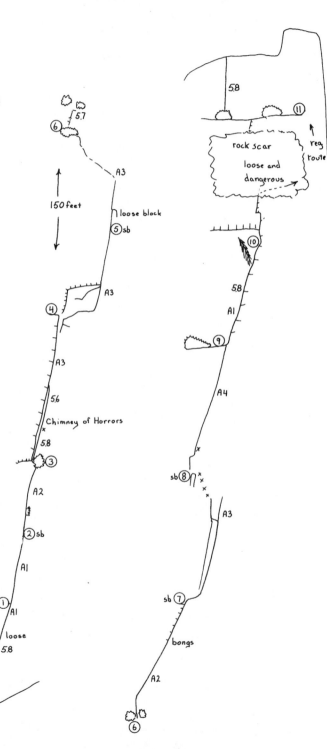

Approach: See page 186.

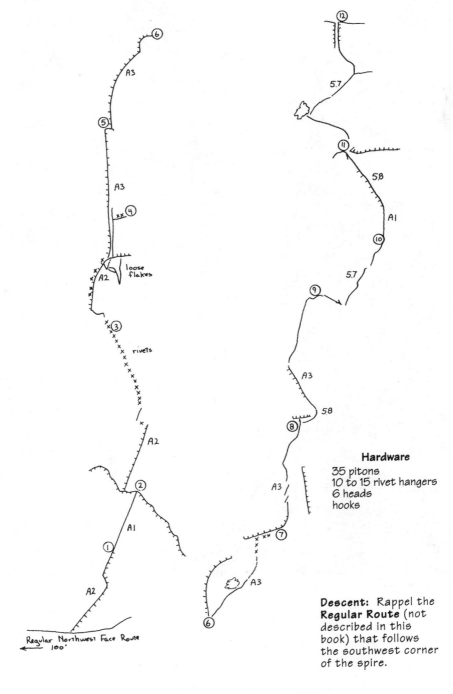

6

A3

5

A3

xx 4

loose
flakes

xx
A2

x 3

rivets

A2

2

A1

1

A2

Regular Northwest Face Route
← 100'

12

5.7

11

5.8

A1

10

5.7

9

A3

5.8

8

A3

7

A3

6

Hardware

35 pitons
10 to 15 rivet hangers
6 heads
hooks

Descent: Rappel the
Regular Route (not
described in this
book) that follows
the southwest corner
of the spire.

Higher Cathedral Rock, East Face

1. Higher Cathedral Spire
2. Lower Cathedral Spire
3. East Face Route
4. Learning to Crawl

Photo on page 188.

Approach: See page 186.
Descent: From the summit of Higher Cathedral Rock walk south and around to the upper part of the Spires Gully.

Hardware

3 KBs
10 LAs
2 ea. ½" and ⅝"
5 ea. ¾" and 1"
4 - 1½"
3 - 2"
2 - 2½"
1 - 3"
nuts
heads
hooks

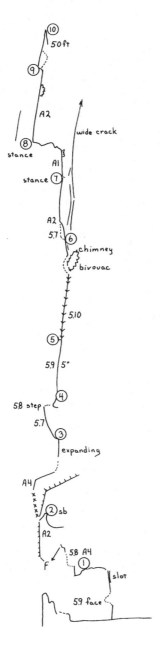

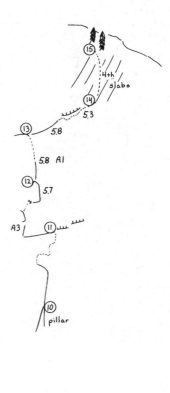

Hardware

1 rurp
15 KBs
15 LAs
2 ea. ½" and ⅝"
3 ea. ¾" and 1"
2 - 1¼"
Friends, 2 ea. to #4

Photo on page 188.

Approach: See page 186.

Descent: From the summit of Higher Cathedral Rock walk south and around to the upper part of the Spires Gully.

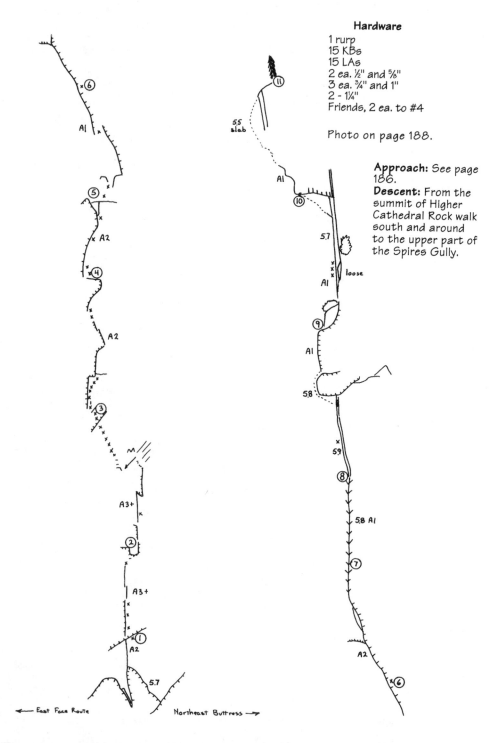

← East Face Route   Northeast Buttress →

Approach: Walk east on the Horse Trail from the long parking turnout near Bridalveil Falls (0.3 miles from the Hwy 41/Hwy 140 junction). Continue up a talus mound to reach the route.

Descent: Scramble down to the Gunsight, the notch between Middle and Lower Cathedral Rocks. A short rappel or two may be necessary in this section.

Hardware
40 pitons, rurps to 4" bong

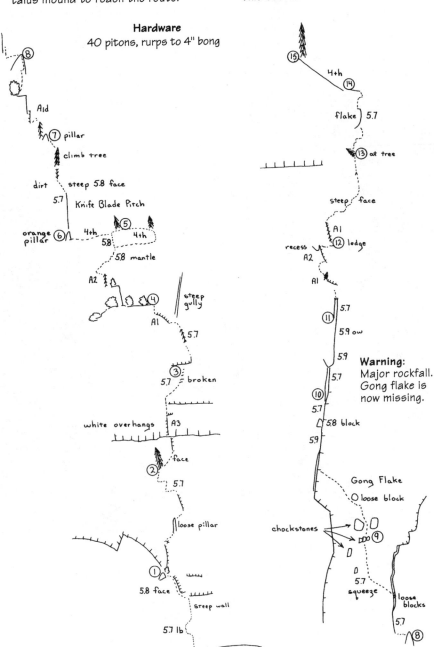

Leaning Tower: West Face

1. Disco Strangler   2. West Face   3. Love Without Anger

Approach: For this and all the routes on the west face of the Leaning Tower, hike up talus above the Bridalveil Falls parking area to gain the Leaning Tower Traverse, the obvious diagonal ledge.

Descent: Two rappels or 4th class lead to scree on the south shoulder. In times of low water it is possible to cross Bridalveil Creek and to descend the Gunsight. Instead, it is common for parties to make a series of rappels down the major chimney system to the south of the Tower (the Leaning Tower Chimney).

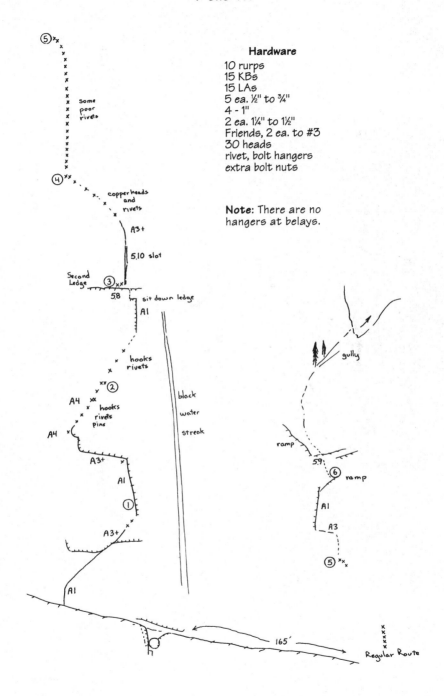

⑤ x x
x
x
x
x
x
x
Some
x **poor**
x **rivets**
x
x
x
x
④ x x
x x
x **copper heads**
x **and**
x **rivets**

A3+

5.10 slot

Second Ledge ③ x x

58 ┤ **sit down ledge**

A1

x **hooks**
x **rivets**
x

x x ②
x x
A4 x x **hooks**
x **rivets**
A4 x **pins**

A3+

A1

①

A3+

A1

black
water
streak

gully

ramp

59
⑥ **ramp**

A1

A3

⑤ x x
x

165'

Regular Route
x
x
x
x
x x x x x

Hardware

10 rurps
15 KBs
15 LAs
5 ea. ½" to ¾"
4 - 1"
2 ea. 1¼" to 1½"
Friends, 2 ea. to #3
30 heads
rivet, bolt hangers
extra bolt nuts

Note: There are no hangers at belays.

Photo on page 192.

Jesus Built My Hotrod
V 5.8 A4

Hardware

15 KBs
15 LAs
3 or 4 beaks
3 ea. baby angles
3 sets TCUs
Friends, 2 sets to #3
15 heads
hooks, all types
nuts

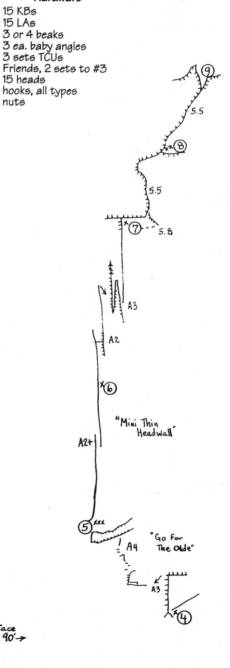

Wet Denim

Ahwahnee Ledge
③

A4- expanding

A3

② ✗

✗

A3

A3

①

A3

West Face
Route 90' →

✗④
A3

⑨

5.5

⑧

5.5

✗⑦ 5.8

A3

A2

✗⑥

"Mini Thin
Headwall"

A2+

⑤ ✗✗✗

"Go For
The Olde"

A4

A3

④

Hardware

West Face
4 LAs
2 ea. ½" to ¾"
Friends, 2 ea. to #2.5
large hook
many small nuts to 2"
wires
heads

**Wet Denim
Daydream (A)**
6 rurps
12 KBs
20 LAs
4 ea. ½" to 1½"
3 - 2"
2 - 2½"
1 - 3"
Friends
hooks
heads

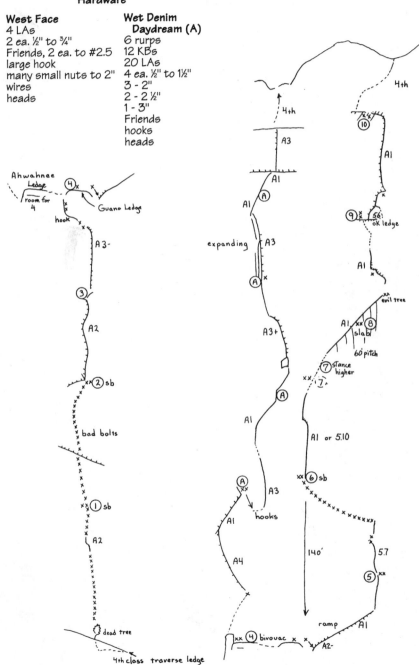

Hardware

5 rurps
15 to 20 KBs
8 bugaboos
20 LAs
3 ea. ½" to ¾"
8 Leepers
1 - 1"
1 - 1¼"
nuts, many tiny to 1"
Friends:
  1 ea. #0.5 to #3
TCUs, 1 ea. #0.4 to
  #0.75
90 heads
hooks, numerous

Note: 140 holes.

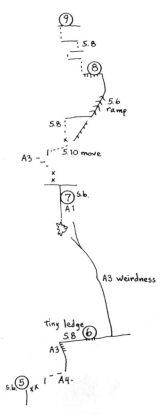

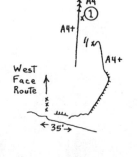

Note: There may be bad
bolts on this route.

A2+/A3

Straight foreward
Fun! Every pitch is good

④ bad bolts

A4+
A2   loose   Black/Blue hybrid Aliens

sb ③   rivets

hooks

A4
A2   hooks

sb ②

A4+
A2

① sb

hooks

A2+/A3   A5

rivets

Regular Route

Large heads, nuts,
50' to bolt
pancake potential hybrid Aliens
4 hook in a row

last large tree

Hardware

10 rurps
KBs, many especially short thin
LAs, many especially short thin
4 ea. ½" and ⅝"
3 - ¾"
2 - 1"
Friends, 2 ea. to #2 Camalot
100 heads, mostly thin   #3 ! 3.5
hooks, all types
crack-n-ups
6 beaks

5
7
8
2
30

All belays new
Stainless 3/8" w/ hangers
Hybrid Aliens

⑧

A1
60°

⑦

ramp?

A3   Aliens
A1

alcove   ⑥   do not touch!

A4

A2

⑤ sb

copperheads
KBs
Beaks
Battle of the Bulge

A2+

Dangling Roof

④

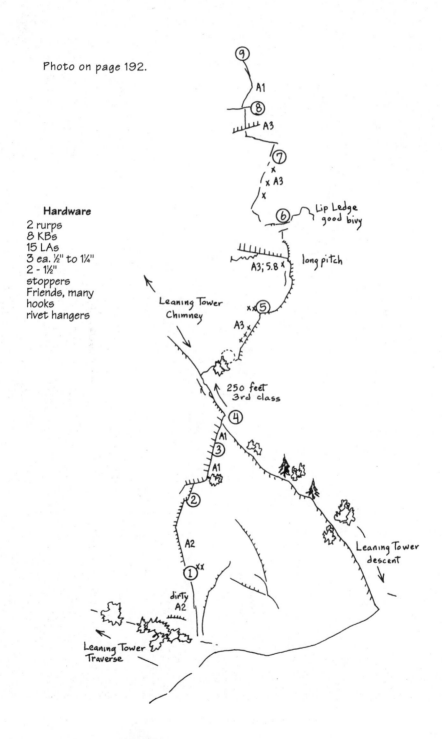

Photo on page 192.

Hardware

2 rurps
8 KBs
15 LAs
3 ea. ½" to 1¼"
2 - 1½"
stoppers
Friends, many
hooks
rivet hangers

9

A1

8

A3

7

x
x A3
x

6 Lip Ledge
good bivy

A3; 5.8 x long pitch

Leaning Tower
Chimney

xx 5

A3 x

250 feet
3rd class

4

A1

3

A1

2

A2

1 xx

dirty
A2

Leaning Tower
Traverse

Leaning Tower
descent

Fifth pitch of **Via sin Aqua**. Photo by Walter J. Flint.

Twelfth pitch of **The Nose**. Photo by Walter J. Flint.

FIRST ASCENTS

RIBBON FALLS
Gold Wall (V, 5.10;A3), Layton Kor and Tom Fender, 5/65
Hole in the Sky (VI, 5.10b;A3), Kevin Fosburg and Paul Turecki, 10/91
West Portal† Chris Fredericks and Steve Roper, 9/63
Rainbows† Ken Boche and Russ McLean, 6/71
Dyslexia (VI, 5.10d;A4), Ellie Hawkins (solo), 8/85
Keel Haul (VI, 5.10;A3), Charlie Porter and Walter Rosenthal, 1972
East Portal† Al Steck, John Evans, Chuck Pratt and Dick Long, 6/64
Solar Power Arête (VI, 5.10a;A3+), Kevin Fosburg and Paul Turecki, 10/91
Gold Ribbon (VI, 5.10;A3), Jim Bridwell and Mike Graham, 5/76
Vain Hope† Royal Robbins, Kim Schmitz and Jim Bridwell, 5/70
Star Drive† Mike Corbett and Steve Bosque, 1983
Crack Me Up† Mike Corbett and Ernie Maylon, 1983

EL CAPITAN
Reach for the Sky† (VI, 5.11;A4+), Jim Beyer, 1989
West Face† TM Herbert and Royal Robbins, 6/67 **FFA** Ray Jardine and
    Bill Price, 5/79
Mr. Midwest (VI, 5.10;A3+), Bill Russell and Doug McDonald, 8/85
Realm of the Flying Monkeys (VI, 5.10a;A3), Steve Bosque and
    Dan McDevitt, 9/85
Mirage (VI, 5.9;A4), Jim Bridwell, Kim Schmitz and Jim Pettigrew, 5/76
Lurking Fear (VI, 5.10;A3), Dave Bircheff and Jim Pettigrew, 5/76
Lost World (VI, 5.10;A3+), Cal Folsom, Dave Anderson and
    Mike Warburton, 4/75
Squeeze Play (VI, 5.10;A3+), Mike Corbett, Gary Edmondson and
    Rich Albuschkat, 4/82
Hole World (VI, 5.10;A4), Eric Kohl, 11/90
West Buttress (VI, 5.10;A3+), Layton Kor and Steve Roper, 1963
For Your Eyes Only (aka Octopussy) (VI, 5.9;A3+), Dan and
    Sue McDevitt, 3/88
Timbauktu Left† (VI, 5.10;A3), Franco Perlotto, 5/88
Never Never Land (VI, 5.9;A4), Bruce Hawkins and Mark Chapman, 1978
Aquarian Wall (VI, 5.9;A4), Jim Bridwell and Kim Schmitz, 6/71
Winds of Change (VI, 5.10;A5), Richard Jensen, 8/91
Wings of Steel (VI, 5.10+;A4), Richard Jensen and Mark Smith, 7/81
Horse Chute (VI, 5.9;A3), Charlie Porter and Hugh Burton, 10/74
Horse Play (VI, 5.9;A3), Steve Grossman and Sue Harrington, 1984
Dihedral Wall (VI, 5.9;A3), Ed Cooper, Jim Baldwin and Glen Denny, 11/62
Cosmos (VI, 5.9;A4), Jim Dunn (solo), 1972 **Direct Finish**, Jim Dunn and
    John Middendorf, 5/90
Excalibur (VI, 5.13a;A4-), Charlie Porter and Hugh Burton, 1975
Bermuda Dunes (VI, 5.11c;A4+), Steve Schneider and John Barbella, 1984
The Heart Route (VI, 5.9;A4), Chuck Kroger and Scott Davis, 4/70
Pacemaker (VI, 5.9;A4), Steve Bosque, Mike Corbett, Murray Barnett
    and Jim Siler, 6/82
Verano Magico† José Luis Gallego and Javier Gallego, 1985
Son of Heart (aka Heart Woute) (VI, 5.10;A3+), Rick Sylvester and
    Claude Wreford-Brown, 1971

Sunkist (VI, 5.9;A4), Bill Price and Dale Bard, 10/78

Jolly Roger (VI, 5.10;A5), Charles Cole and Steve Grossman, 1979

Magic Mushroom (VI, 5.10;A4), Hugh Burton and Steve Sutton, 5/72

The Shield (VI, 5.9;A3+), Charlie Porter and Gary Bocarde, 1972

Dorn Direct (VI, 5.9;A4), Tony Yaniro and Ron Olevsky, 6/77

False Shield† Charles Cole, 5/84

Turning Point† Steve Grossman, 5/84

Muir Wall (VI, 5.10;A3), Yvon Chouinard and TM Herbert, 6/65

Salathé Wall (VI, 5.13b), Royal Robbins, Chuck Pratt and Tom Frost, 9/61
    FFA Todd Skinner and Paul Piana, 1988

Triple Direct (VI, 5.9;A2), Jim Bridwell and Kim Schmitz, 1969

Meditteraneo Miguel Angel Gallego, José Luis Gallego, Javier Gallego
    and Carlos Gallego, 1981

Grape Race (VI, 5.9;A4), Charlie Porter and Bev Johnson, 5/74

The Nose (VI, 5.11;A2), Warren Harding, Wayne Merry and George
    Whitmore, 11/58 **Free variations to Camp IV**, Ray Jardine et al, 1980

The Central Scrutinizer† (VI, 5.11c;A4+), Steve Grossman and Jay Ladin, 8/88

The Real Nose (VI, 5.10;A4), Charles Cole and Steve Grossman, 1984

Tribal Rite† Walter Rosenthal, Tom Carter and Alan Bard, 10/78

Genesis (VI, 5.11b;A4+), Doug Englekirk and Eric Brand, 5/89

New Dawn (VI, 5.9;A4), Yvon Chouinard, Chuck Pratt, Dennis Hennek
    and Chris Jones (complete route) Charlie Porter, 1972

Mescalito (VI, 5.9;A4)Charlie Porte, Hugh Burton, Steve Sutton and
    Chris Nelson, 10/73

Hockey Night in Canada (VI, 5.10;A3), Perry Beckham, Scott Flavelle,
    Dave Lane, 5/80

Space (VI, 5.10;A4+), Charles Cole, 7/85

South Seas (VI, 5.8;A4+), Bill Price, Charlie Row and Guy Thompson, 9/79

Pacific Ocean Wall (VI, 5.9;A4), Jim Bridwell, Bill Westbay, Jay Fiske
    and Fred East, 5/75

Sea of Dreams (VI, 5.9;A5), Jim Bridwell, Dale Bard and
    Dave Diegelman, 10/78

North America Wall (VI, 5.8;A3), Tom Frost, Yvon Chouinard, Chuck Pratt
    and Royal Robbins, 10/64

Wyoming Sheep Ranch (VI, 5.9;A5+), Rob Slater and John Barbella, 8/84

Heartland (VI, 5.10;A4+), John Barbella and Eric Brand, 8/87

New Jersey Turnpike (VI, 5.10;A4+),Bruce Hawkins, Ron Kauk, Dale Bard
    and Hugh Burton, 4/77

Atlantic Ocean Wall (VI, 5.10;A5), John Middendorf and John Barbella, 9/85

Iron Hawk (VI, 5.9;A4), Dale Bard and Ron Kauk, 9/78

Native Son (VI, 5.9;A4+), Walt Shipley and Troy Johnson, 8/87

Scorched Earth (VI, 5.11;A5), Randy Leavitt and Rob Slater, 8/87

Aurora (VI, 5.8;A5), Peter Mayfield and Greg Child, 9/81

Tangerine Trip (VI, 5.9;A3+), Charlie Porter and John-Paul de St.Croix, 1973

Virginia† (VI, 5.7;A3), Chuck Clance and Steve Bosque, 7/92

Lost in America (VI, 5.9;A5), Randy Leavitt and Greg Child, 1985

Zenyatta Mondatta (VI, 5.7;A5), Jim Bridwell, Peter Mayfield and
    Charlie Row, 9/81

The Shortest Straw (VI, 5.10;A3+), Rick Lovelace (solo), 3/90

Zodiac (VI, 5.11;A3+), Charlie Porter, 11/72

Surgeon General (VI, 5.9;A5), Eric Kohl and Walt Shipley, 5/90
Lunar Eclipse (VI, 5.10;A4), John Barbella and Steve Schneider, 7/82
Born Under a Bad Sign (VI, 5.10;A5), Bill Price and Tim Washick, 1979
Plastic Surgery Disaster (VI, 5.8;A5), Eric Kohl (solo), 6/91
Bad Seed (VI, 5.9;A4+), Bill Russell and Troy Johnson, 10/88
Bad to the Bone (VI, 5.9+;A4), Jay Smith and Lidija Painkiher, 8/84
Eagle's Way (VI, 5.10;A4), Mark Chapman, Mike Graham and Jim Orey, 1976
On the Waterfront (VI, 5.9;A5), Steve Bosque, Mike Corbett and Gwen Schneider, 8/86
High Plains Dripper (VI, 5.11;A5), Eric Kohl and Alan Humphrey, 7/89
Pressure Cooker (VI, 5.10;A4), Eric Kohl (solo), 7/90
Get Whacked (VI, 5.10;A5), Eric Kohl (solo), 6/92
Waterfall Route (VI, 5.10;A4), Darryl Teske and T. Polk, 10/75
Chinese Water Torture (VI, 5.11;A4), Karl McConachie and Jay Smith, 7/81
Snake† Knez Franek and Walace, 5/83

YOSEMITE FALLS
Forbidden Wall† Warren Harding, Dave Lomba, Christie Tewes and Steve Bosque, Summer 1978
Wheel of Torture (VI, 5.7;A4), Eric Kohl (solo), 10/89
World of Pain (VI, 5.8;A5), Eric Kohl (solo), 9/91
Via sin Aqua (VI, 5.10;A2), Rick Sylvester and Bugs McKeith, 9/70
Via sin Liquor (VI, 5.9;A4), Eric Kohl and Alan Humphrey, 10/88
Miscreant Wall (V, 5.9;A4), Bruce Hawkins and Keith Nannery, 1973
Misty Wall (V, 5.11d;A0), Dick McCracken and Royal Robbins, 6/63
    FFA (less pendulums) Walt Shipley and Kevin Fosburg, 1991
Electric Ocean (VI, 5.10;A4), Eric Kohl (solo), 4/92
Reckless Abandon (VI, 5.8;A4+), Eric Kohl (solo), 2/91
Aqua Vulva (VI, 5.10;A4), Eric Kohl and John Middendorf, 11/89
Dante's Inferno (VI, 5.9;A3+), Eric Kohl (solo), 6/89
Lost Arrow Spire, Direct Route (V, 5.11;A3), Warren Harding and Pat Callis, 6/68
Lost Arrow Tip (5.12b or 5.8 ;A2), Fritz Lippmann, Jack Arnold, Anton Nelson and Robin Hansen, 9/46 FFA Dave Schultz et al, 5/84
Yosemite Pointless (V, 5.9;A3), Bob Ost and Norman Boles, 5/86
Rainbow (V, 5.10;A3), Paul Fida and Chris Freel, 1983
Seand Paradise† Knez Francek and Freser Marjan, 4/82
Czech Route (V, 5.10;A3), Jan Porvazik and A. Behia, 10/78

ROYAL ARCHES
Die Schweine von Oben (VI, 5.11;A3+), Bill Russell and Paul Fida, 1983
Toxic Waste Dump (VI, 5.8;A3+), Eric Kohl (solo), 12/89
Rhombus Wall Warren Hardine et al, 1975
Arches Direct† Royal Robbins and Joe Fitschen, 6/60
Bulging Puke (V, 5.10;A4), Bill Russell and Chris Friel, 11/81

WASHINGTON COLUMN
South Central (V, 5.10a;A2), Jim Bridwell and Joe Faint, 10/67
Southern Man (V, 5.8;A2), Francis Ross and Rich Albushkat, 1992

South Face (V, 5.10a;A2), Layton Kor and Chris Fredericks, 6/64
Skull Queen (V, 5.10;A3), Jeff Altenburg, Chuck Clance and Steve Bosque, 6/84
The Re-animator (VI, 5.8;A4), Eric Kohl and Walt Shipley, 1/90 **(Note:** Rivets added on pitches 7 and 8 by 2nd ascent.)
The Prow (V, 5.10a;A2), Royal Robbins and Glen Denny, 5/69
Ten Days After (VI, 5.9;A3), John Barbella and Eric Brand, 2/87
Electric Lady Land (VI, 5.10a;A4), Gib Lewis, Rick Accomazzo and Richard Harrison, 5/75
Horney/Johnson (VI, 5.10;A3+), Jeff Hornibrook and Troy Johnson, 10/88
Mideast Crisis (V, 5.8;A4), Steve Bosque and Mike Corbett, 4/83
Saddam Hussein (V, 5.9;A4), Eric Brand and Stewart Irving, 9/90
Great Slab Route (V, 5.8;A4), Layton Kor, Jim Madsen and Kim Schmitz, 5/67
Bad Wall† (VI, 5.8;A4) Jim Madsen and Kim Schmitz, 1967

MT. WATKINS

Hook, Line and Sinker (VI, 5.10;A3+), Mike Munger, Angus Thuermer and Steve Larson, 5/78
South Face Route (VI, 5.9;A3), Warren Harding, Yvon Chouinard and Chuck Pratt, 7/64
Tenaya's Terror (VI, 5.9;A4), Mike Corbett and Steve Bosque, 6/85
The Prism (VI, 5.10;A3+), Urmas Franosch and Sean Plunkett, 8/92
Bob Locke Memorial Buttress (VI, 5.11;A4), Jim Bridwell, Ron Kauk, John Long and Kim Schmitz, 10/78
Escape from Freedom (V, 5.11c;A1), Urmas Franosch and Bruce Morris, 6/28/92 to 7/4/92

EAST QUARTER DOME:
Nashville Skyline† (V, 5.8;A3), Charlie Porter and Gary Bocarde, 7/72
North Face (V, 5.9;A2), Yvon Chouinard and Tom Frost, 9/62
    FFA (Pegasus) Max Jones and Mark Hudon, 1980
Route of All Evil (V, 5.9;A4), Matt Donohoe and Cliff Jennings, 1971

WEST QUARTER DOME:
North Face (V, 5.8;A3), Phil Koch and Dave Goeddel, 9/69

HALF DOME

Northwest Buttress (IV 5.8;A3), Andy Embick and Bob Jensen, 9/69
Regular Northwest Face (VI, 5.9;A2), Royal Robbins, Jerry Gallwas and Mike Sherrick, 7/57 **FFA** Jim Erickson and Art Higbee, 1976
Arcturas (VI, 5.7;A4), Royal Robbins and Dick Dorworth, 7/70
Same As It Never Was† Karl McConachie, Jay Smith and Randy Grandstaff, 7/86
Direct Northwest Face (VI, 5.10;A3+), Royal Robbins and Dick McCracken, 6/63
Queen of Spades (VI, 5.9;A4), Charles Cole, 7/84
Shadows† (VI, A5), Jim Bridwell, Cito Kirkpatrick, Charlie Row and Billy Westbay, 1989
The Vodka Putsch† (VI, 5.10;A4), Bill Russell and Pete Takeda
Tis-sa-ack (VI, 5.10;A4), Royal Robbins and Don Peterson, 10/69

The Kali Yuga (VI, 5.10;A4), Walt Shipley and John Middendorf, 10/89
Zenith (VI, 5.9;A4), Jim Bridwell and Kim Schmitz, 1978
The White Room (VI, 5.10;A4), Sean Plunkett and Walt Shipley, 9/88
The Big Chill (VI, 5.9;A4), Jim Bridwell, Peter Mayfield, Sean Plunkett
    and Steve Bosque, 8/87
The Promised Land† (VI, 5.10;A4) Kevin Fosburg, Jeff Hornibrook and
    Troy Johnson, 9/89
Arctic Sea (VI, 5.10;A4), Tom Cosgrove and Duane Raleigh, 1983
Bushido (VI, 5.10;A4), Jim Bridwell and Dale Bard, 10/77
The Jet Stream (VI, 5.9;A4), Sean Plunkett and Bill Russell, 9/89

DIVING BOARD:
The Luminescent Wall (VI, 5.10b;A4), John Barbella and Walt Shipley, 6/87
Porcelain Wall† Warren Harding, Dave Lomba and Steve Bosque, mid-'70s

SOUTH FACE:
Lost Again (VI, 5.10;A3+), Eric Kohl (solo), 1972
South Face Route (VI, 5.8;A3), Warren Harding and Galen Rowell, 7/70
Southern Belle (V, 5.12d), Walt Shipley and Dave Schultz, 6/87
    FFA Dave Schultz and Scott Cosgrove, 1988
Karma (V, 5.11d;A0), Dave Schultz, Ken Yager and Jim Campbell, 7/86

LIBERTY CAP
West Buttress (V, 5.10;A3), Mike Corbett, Steve Bosque, 12/85
Southwest Face (VI, 5.10;A3), Galen Rowell, Joe Faint and
    Warren Harding, 5/69
Direct Southwest Face (VI, 5.10;A5), Werner Braun and Rick Cashner, 5/82
Turkey Shoot† (V, 5.9;A3), Ken Yager and Steve Bosque, 1/88
A Joint Adventure (IV 5.9;A3+), Paul Gagner, Karl McConachie and
    John Barbella, 7/79

PANORAMA CLIFF
Bananarama (V, 5.10a;A3), Rich Albuschkat, Steve Bosque and
    Murray Barnett, 8/89

GLACIER POINT, 9 O'CLOCK WALL:
Ice Age (VI, 5.8;A5), Eric Kohl (solo), 7/90
Crystal Cyclone (VI, A4+), Eric Kohl (solo), 7/91
Time Machine (VI, A5+), Bob Shonerd (solo), 10/84

SENTINEL
Kor-Denny Route† Layton Kor and Glen Denny, 6/63
Psychedelic Wall† Ken Boche and Dennis Hennek, 9/66
Flashback (V, 5.8;A3), Steve Bosque and Rich Albuschkat, 10/89
Direct North Face (V, 5.9;A3), Royal Robbins and Tom Frost, 5/62
Gobi Wall (V, 5.8;A4), Chuck Pratt and Ken Boche, 7/69
Flying Buttress Direct (V, 5.9;A2), Chris Fredericks and Layton Kor, 6/65
In Cold Blood (V, 5.11b;A3), Royal Robbins, 5/70

CATHEDRAL

HIGHER SPIRE:
Northwest Face (V, 5.8;A3), Tom Frost and Royal Robbins, 6/61
Higher Aspirations(V, 5.8;A3), Rik Derrick and Steve Bosque, 11/82

HIGHER ROCK:
East Face Route (V, 5.10;A4), Jim Bridwell and Chris Fredericks, 6/67
Learning to Crawl (V, 5.9;A3+), Mike Corbett, Steve Bosque and
    Fritz Fox, 1985

LOWER ROCK:
North Face (V, 5.9;A3), Joe Fitschen, Chuck Pratt and Royal Robbins, 6/60

LEANING TOWER
Disco Strangler (V, 5.10;A4), Earl Redfern, Tom Bepler and Eric Brand, 3/85
Jesus Built My Hotrod (V, 5.8;A4), Eric Kohl and Eric Rasmussen, 9/92
Wet Denim Daydream (V, 5.7;A4), Darrell Hatton and
    Angus Thuermer, 1977
West Face (V, 5.7;A3), Warren Harding primarily with Glen Denny
    and Al MacDonald, 1961
Heading for Oblivion (VI, 5.10;A4+), Jim Beyer, 1986
Roulette (VI, A5), Earl Redfern and Tom Bepler, 3/84

B.O.L.T. WALL (BROTHER OF LEANING TOWER):
Love Without Anger (V, 5.8;A3), Steve Bosque and Rich Albuschkat, 10/88

FFA "First free ascent"
† Topo of route is *not* provided for this entry.

We request that all corrections, as well as new route information, be sent to the authors, in care of Chockstone Press, PO Box 3505, Evergreen Colorado, 80439. Please include the following information:

1. Provide the NAME of the route, the RATING (try to use a, b, c, or d rather than plus or minus), the approximate DATE of the first ascent, and the FULL NAMES of the first ascent party.

2. If the route lies adjacent to an existing route, give directions or reference in relation to that route. Be sure to include the route name and page number (for reference).

3. If you have a photograph of the route, please photocopy it and mark the line taken by the route including the location of any bolts or fixed gear.

4. A topo of the route is vital. You may wish to photograph the topo in this guide which covers the appropriate section of rock and draw the topo on the photocopy.

Again, the best way to make sure that new route information reaches the authors is to mail it to them, in care of Chockstone Press, PO Box 3505, Evergreen Colorado, 80439. We appreciate your assistance.

Page numbers in **bold** represent
  photographs.

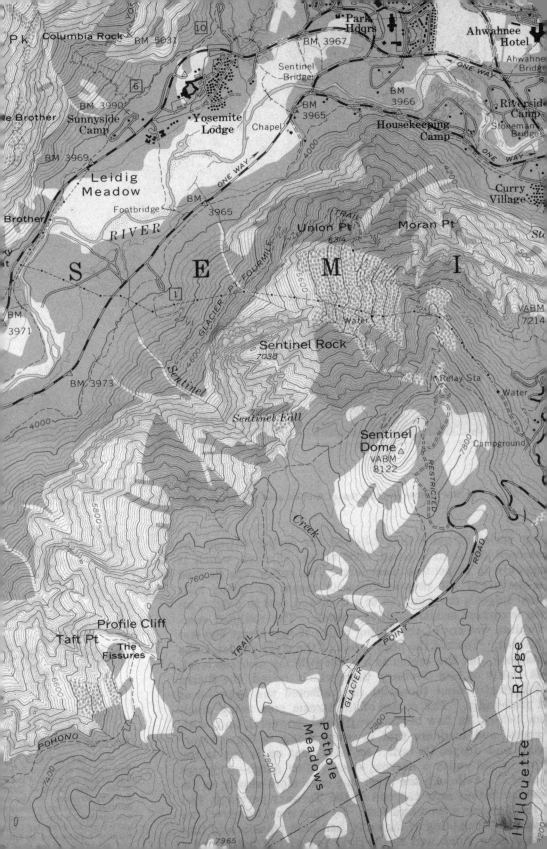

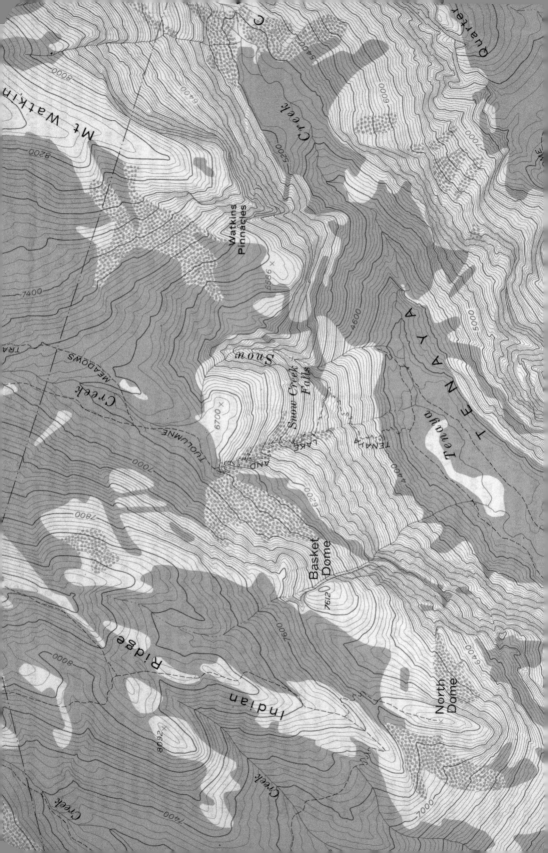

Access: It's everybody's concern

the ACCESS FUND

THE ACCESS FUND, a national, non-profit climbers' organization, is working to keep you climbing. The Access Fund helps preserve access and protect the environment by providing funds for land acquisitions and climber support facilities, financing scientific studies, publishing educational materials promoting low-impact climbing, and providing start-up money, legal counsel and other resources to local climbers' coalitions.

Climbers can help preserve access by being responsible users of climbing areas. Here are some practical ways to support climbing:

- **COMMIT YOURSELF TO "LEAVING NO TRACE."** Pick up litter around campgrounds and the crags. Let your actions inspire others.

- **DISPOSE OF HUMAN WASTE PROPERLY.** Use toilets whenever possible. If none are available, choose a spot at least 50 meters from any water source. Dig a hole 6 inches (15 cm) deep, and bury your waste in it. *Always pack out toilet paper* in a "Zip-Lock"-type bag.

- **UTILIZE EXISTING TRAILS.** Avoid cutting switchbacks and trampling vegetation.

- **USE DISCRETION WHEN PLACING BOLTS AND OTHER "FIXED" PROTECTION.** Camouflage all anchors with rock-colored paint. Use chains for rappel stations, or leave rock-colored webbing.

- **RESPECT RESTRICTIONS THAT PROTECT NATURAL RESOURCES AND CULTURAL ARTIFACTS.** Appropriate restrictions can include prohibition of climbing around Indian rock art, pioneer inscriptions, and on certain formations during raptor nesting season. Power drills are illegal in wilderness areas. *Never chisel or sculpt holds in rock on public lands, unless it is expressly allowed* – no other practice so seriously threatens our sport.

- **PARK IN DESIGNATED AREAS,** not in undeveloped, vegetated areas. Carpool to the crags!

- **MAINTAIN A LOW PROFILE.** Other people have the same right to undisturbed enjoyment of natural areas as do you.

- **RESPECT PRIVATE PROPERTY.** Don't trespass in order to climb.

- **JOIN OR FORM A GROUP TO DEAL WITH ACCESS ISSUES IN YOUR AREA.** Consider clean-ups, trail building or maintenance, or other "goodwill" projects.

- **JOIN THE ACCESS FUND.** To become a member, *simply make a donation (tax-deductible) of any amount.* Only by working together can we preserve the diverse American climbing experience.

The Access Fund. Preserving America's diverse climbing resources.
The Access Fund • P.O. Box 17010 • Boulder, CO 80308